PUPPY NUR
RAISING YOUR PUPPY WITH LOVE

Shay Kelly, MSc.

Copyright © 2023 SHAY KELLY
All rights reserved. No part of this book may be reproduced, stored, or transmitted in any form without written permission from the author.

Limits of Liability and Disclaimer of Warranty: The author shall not be liable in the event of incidental or consequential damages or loss in connection with or arising out of the furnishings, performance, or use of the suggestions or instructions contained in this book.

ISBN: 9798389513860

If you find typographical errors in this book, give your puppy a treat so at least some good comes of my ineptness.

Dedicated to my beloved Barney (aka Mr B). A piece of my heart will be forever missing.

Contents

Introduction	1
Coming Home	4
Food	5
Treats	8
Bowls	10
Cleaning Products	11
Heartbeat Warming Pillow or Stuffed Animal	11
Collar & Tag	11
Harness & Leash	12
Why I Don't Walk Dogs by Their Collar	13
Home Environment	16
First Nights	19
Crates & Pens	23
Crate/Pen Training	25
Life Stages	27
Body Language	35
Stretching, Scratching, and Sniffing	36
Yawning, Looking away, Tongue flicks, Lip licking	36
Eyes	37
Mouth	38
Ears	39
Raised Paw	39
Shake Off	39
Low Body Posture	40
Tail	40
Attention Seeking	42
Sometimes It's Hard	45
Consider the Relationship	46
How Dogs Learn	50
Capturing & Default Behaviour	55
Toilet Training	57
Puppy Biting/Mouthing	62
Chewing	66
What's in a Name	73
Socialisation & Habituation	78
Introductions	81

Socialisation with Dogs	82
Anthropomorphism & Emotions	84
The Vacuum Cleaner & Other Exciting Things	89
Destroying Their Toys	91
Training, sort of!	95
Leave it/Drop it	98
Swap it – Drop it	100
Wait (your emergency stop)	102
Not Jumping Up	106
Recall	109
Checking in	117
Walking Together	119
300 Peck	125
A Time for Silence	127
Agency	130
Opportunities to Increase Agency	132
Enrichment (enjoying puppyhood)	136
Settle	145
Preventing Separation Anxiety	149
Fireworks	155
Resource Guarding	158
Twenty Things Your Pup Desperately Wants to Tell You	161
The Final Word	163

Introduction

Legally speaking we own the dog, and this often causes them to be treated like property. However, the dog was never consulted about this arrangement. Dogs have no way of understanding that we've collectively decided that they're our property. The dog doesn't understand ownership, the dog understands relationship! For the dog, life is pretty much all about relationships – relationships with their human, relationships with other dogs, and relationships with their environments.

To understand the dog, we must try to see life from their perspective. We are not dogs, so seeing life from their perspective might seem impossible. After all, we can't even truly perceive life from the perspective of another human. What two people see when they stand side by side and look out at the vista will be a little different from one another. Moreso, their feelings about the experience will differ. Some people spot an Aston Martin motor car and are filled with awe; others may feel similar emotions from looking at a sunset, and many others will not even notice either one.

If we cannot perceive how other humans see the world, how can we possibly see life from a dog's world view? We can't – not entirely, but we can at least try. That's what I've tried to do throughout this book, and it's what I try to do throughout all my dog training and behaviour work. We know from the dedicated work of Jaak Panksepp (1943–2017), a neuroscientist, specialising in emotions, that we share the same primary emotional circuits with other animals. The study of emotions (or affective neuroscience, in academic circles) was often criticised, mainly due to the dominant belief in behaviourism, popularised by scientists such as B.F. Skinner, which considers learning only from the perspective of reward and punishment. Basically, this means that any given behaviour is more likely to reoccur if it is rewarded (reinforced), and less likely to reoccur if it is punished (by an unpleasant event). Behaviourism doesn't consider emotions whatsoever, which is a great shame because emotions are the driving force behind behaviour. Nowadays, it is becoming increasingly accepted that emotions and emotional wellbeing play a vital role in animal behaviour.

Consider why you do any of the things you do. There is always an underlying emotional feeling. If we didn't have these feelings, we wouldn't bother to look for anything we need, we'd never get angry, or frightened; we wouldn't nurture our children, or grieve our friends; we'd never procreate, and we wouldn't ever play. We wouldn't do anything at all. We are motivated to do everything we do by how we feel about it. The circuits Panksepp identified are SEEKING (enthusiasm and anticipation), RAGE (anger), FEAR (anxiety), LUST (sexual arousal), CARE (nurture), GRIEF, (sadness), and PLAY (joy).

It's been a long journey, but today it is clear that dogs are sentient beings, motivated by the same primary emotions as us. Understanding just this is enough to give us a glimpse into their perspectives and experiences. If we want to influence and guide our dog's behaviour, what better way than to consider their emotional relationship with the world around them? What better way than to see, or at least try to see, life from the dog's perspective?

There are many books about dog training and about raising puppies. The problem is that many are not based on ethical practices or scientific learning theory. They're often based on personal beliefs and punishing dogs to prevent unwanted behaviour. This book is written from my own personal experiences, but it's also based on my knowledge of scientific behaviour principles gained during many years of academic study. I'm grateful you chose this book from the many hundreds you might have reached for – I hope it helps on the journey ahead; I hope it makes a difference for you and your wonderful dog.

Throughout the book I will refer to Monty, my new Labrador puppy and let you know how he's getting along and how we deal with any issues. It's a great help to have Monty at my side. He keeps me grounded in the realities of raising a puppy – I'm not just describing what you should do, I'm coming along for the ride, assisted by the greatest dog behaviour expert there is: the dog.

COMING HOME

Why are you reading this book? Probably because you're planning on getting a new puppy, or perhaps you already have your new puppy. Either way, congratulations! Getting a new puppy is always such an exciting time for us. We're usually counting down the days to when we can bring them home. It's the dawning of a new adventure. But what is it like from the pup's perspective? It must surely be overwhelming, confusing, and downright scary. They woke up in the only home they've known, completely unaware of how life was about to suddenly change. Not a little change, but a complete change. By evening, everything will look and smell very different. The humans they knew will be gone, replaced by new ones. The mother they ran to for safety will no longer be there for them, and the littermates they so eagerly played with, chased, and snuggled up with – all gone!

Well, that may be the saddest start to a puppy book you'll ever see – but don't worry, we can put things right. You can be a home worth leaving all that behind for. You can be a home where the pup's needs and perspectives are considered. You can be the pup's new place of safety. You can be the pup's new family, help them settle in, feel safe, and have fun. You can give your puppy a really good life in a loving and safe environment. Imagine all the different people they could have ended up with, but here they are with you. It's an awesome privilege to have such a degree of influence over the life of another sentient being. So let's get started.

The first consideration is settling them into their new life. If you've not collected your puppy yet, consider giving a blanket to the breeder so it can be placed in with the pups and the mother for a few days. This will give you something with a familiar comforting scent to bring home with your puppy. It's in no way the same as having their mother and littermates, but it is at least something familiar – something which feels safe. The next thing to do is to ensure you have everything you might need.

Food
Bowls
Cleaning products
Collar and tag
Heartbeat warming pillow or stuffed animal
Harness and leash
Puppy crate or pen, if you intend to use one (see crates and pens section)
Puppy pads (if you want to use them)
Toys
Things to chew (see section on chewing)

Food

Usually, the puppy's breeder will supply some food with the pup. It's probably a good idea to stick with what they've already been eating, at least for a couple of weeks. This will be familiar to them, reducing stress and the chances of an upset stomach. But then comes the big decision, what to feed your dog. This, I'm sorry to say, is a minefield. The dog training world is very divided on the subject of diet. I don't know of a single diet that would not be condemned by others of a different persuasion. There seems to be more arguments about what we feed dogs than about what we feed children. Before we go any further, I should make it clear that I'm a dog behaviour expert; I'm not a dog nutritionist. For this reason, I stay away from recommending any particular food type or recipe. Options include kibble, tinned, dehydrated, raw, home cooked, and cooked (delivered in packs). There is a huge range of price and quality, especially so for kibble. Kibble is certainly easy to store and feed, but from the dog's perspective, I'm sceptical that they'd ever choose it over fresh ingredients. Moist and meaty foods tend to be a dog's preferred choice.

In the end, I think we should all do the best we can manage. Currently, my personal choice is to prepare home cooked food, but you do need to do a little research into appropriate recipes. *BalanceIT.com* is a useful resource for people wishing to home prepare their dog's food. Feeding is such a minefield that it can become stressful worrying if we are doing the right thing. Some foods can be very expensive, and even then we don't know if we are doing the right thing. It's important that we do not pressure ourselves or feel pressured by others to provide a diet which is outside of our budget. In life, we often have to compromise on ideals, and this is no different than when we are feeding ourselves. You should not feel any sense of shame for feeding a budget brand dog food – the most important thing is that your dog is fed, loved and respected.

Raw feeding has become more popular over recent years and the people who feed it are often passionate advocates of its benefits. There are different options available; for example, home prepared recipes, complete frozen meals, and freeze-dried complete meals. However, the many health benefit claims are supported only anecdotally at present. There are concerns over the safety of feeding a raw diet, and it is not supported by the majority of veterinarians. The concern is regarding the likelihood of raw foods containing pathogenic bacteria. For example, van Bree et al. (2018) analysed 35 commercial raw meat-based diets for zoonotic bacterial and parasitic pathogens:

8 (23%) contained Escherichia coli

28 (80%) contained extended-spectrum beta-lactamases-producing E coli

19 (54%) contained listeria monocytogenes

15 (43%) contained other listeria species

7 (20%) contained salmonella

4 (11%) contained Sarcocystis cruzi

4 (11%) contained S tenella

2 (6%) contained Toxoplasma gondii.

These statistics look a little scary, but I know many people who have fed raw diets for years without any issues. For those who feed raw meat-based diets it may be prudent to substantiate the quality control procedures of the producer. I've considered feeding a raw diet many times, but I'm not yet fully convinced of the benefit over risk. On the plus side, Algya et al. (2018) found lightly cooked food to be significantly more digestible than raw; therefore, I will stick with this method until I'm persuaded otherwise. If you're interested in learning more about this subject, I highly recommend the books of canine nutritionist, Linda P Case.

Treats

When I'm working with dogs, I tend to use a lot of food treats. There are thousands of different dog treats on the market, from the very cheap to the ridiculously expensive, and it's often difficult to ascertain the quality of the product. Hotdogs/frankfurters are a common choice because they are easy to chop into small pieces and are relatively cheap to purchase. However, they're something humans shouldn't eat too much of (high in saturated fats and highly processed), so feeding them to our dogs might also be suspect. I've used them in the past, but these days, I prefer to buy chicken breast or a piece of beef; I cook it, and chop it up into fingernail size pieces. I also use freeze-dried meat treats. A third option is to make meaty treats by drying out very thin meat slices in a food dehydrator, but this is usually a lengthy process of around 10 hours, depending on your dehydrator and the meat used.

Dog guardians are sometimes concerned about the use of food to train their dog. Some think of it as bribery. Others feel that the dog should want to perform behaviour just because they've been asked to. However, food is a primary reinforcer – every one of the millions of ancestors of your dog had something in common; they were motivated to find food.

All animals, in the wild, spend a considerable amount of their time gaining enough food to survive. If we feed all of the dog's required daily calories from a bowl, and use no food for training or enrichment, we take away part of an animal's natural behaviour of seeking food. Food is essential to life. But the opportunity to seek or earn food is equally important.

The brain's dopamine levels peak when we're engaged in opportunities which lead to getting something we want. It's not the reinforcement (getting what we wanted) that creates the feel-good factor, it's the pursuit of it. From an evolutionary perspective, this makes perfect sense. The willingness to engage in opportunities to gain food is key to survival. Animals don't tend to sit around waiting for food to turn up and jump into their mouth.

Using food to train dogs helps to eliminate the behaviour void which is left behind due to them not needing to find their own food. Using food allows them to enjoy life by switching on that seeking system and giving them the opportunity to gain reinforcers. We're creating desire and igniting their brain. We're also creating a good bond between ourselves and the dog. Each time we reinforce behaviour with food, we're creating pleasant associations and strengthening our relationship.

There are some caveats to using food in dog training and enrichment. Firstly, it's important to keep our dogs at a healthy weight – any food used for training or enrichment should be considered when calculating their meals. Enrichment feeding and training with food, does not require extra food; it requires that we are more creative with their daily food allowance. The second caveat is that our relationship with the puppy should not be all about food. There's always a bigger picture. The pup also needs play, safety, comfort, companionship, etc. Treats don't always need to be made of food; for example, many dogs will enjoy playing tug, chasing a ball, or playing with their favourite toy.

Bowls

How could you go wrong with choosing food and water bowls? It can't go too far wrong, but from experience, plastic bowls are easily chewed and stainless steel bowls are sometimes not liked by dogs because of their reflectiveness, especially if they are used for water. These bowls are also very easily knocked over. With this in mind, I usually opt for the large, weighty, porcelain bowls. It is important to wash food bowls thoroughly after each use, and wash water bowls daily.

We would not eat or drink from dirty vessels, and nor should our dogs.

Cleaning products

The better you are at watching the puppy, the less you will need to clean up those little accidents, but just in case, get an enzymatic, pet friendly, stain and odour remover, specifically designed for urine. This helps to prevent the puppy recognising the same spot and repeating the error. There are literally hundreds on the market. I actually bought two bottles, and didn't need them, but Monty's the first dog to be this damn good at toilet training.

Heartbeat warming pillow or stuffed animal

These simply provide a little comfort by replicating the heartbeat of the pup's mother. However, they are not always accepted by pups, and I've known a few who were a little distressed by heartbeat pillows; make sure they're comfortable with it before giving it to them to sleep with. Don't fall into the trap of believing we can simply replace the pup's old family with a few clever products – their old family can only be replaced by their new family, and that's us.

Collar and tag

I'm not a big fan of collars but UK law states that the dog must wear a collar and tag when you're on public property. This is in addition to being microchipped. The tag must contain the owner's name and address, including postcode (zip code). It's probably wise to have your phone number on there too and most people opt for the dog's name on the reverse. The downside to the collar is that it can become snagged, trapping the dog, or causing them to panic. Additionally, if you have more than one dog, jaws can become stuck under the collar of the other dog, especially if they play together. For this reason I don't advise leaving the collar on when dogs are unsupervised at home. However, things are never so simple – if the dog was ever to escape the home, perhaps through a door, accidentally left open, you would want them to have their tag on, making it easier and quicker for them to be returned by a good Samaritan.

Harness and leash

Harnesses make walking on a leash more comfortable for the dog and prevent damage to the dog's neck, which may come from pulling on a traditional collar. Some harnesses have a Y shaped front section, for example, Truelove and Perfect-fit brands. Others have a breast strap, horizontally crossing the chest; for example, the JuliusK9 brand. Recently, the Y shaped harness has grown in popularity. Some concerns have been raised about the possibility of other designs restricting shoulder movement. I'm not yet convinced of this but as a precaution, I moved to the Y shaped harnesses some years back. Whatever you choose, please ensure it is not one designed to tighten if the dog pulls; these are designed to make pulling uncomfortable – if being uncomfortable worked to stop pulling, you wouldn't see so many dogs pulling on a traditional collar. Making the dog uncomfortable, as we will discuss later in the book, will likely lead to other behavioural problems.

The obvious problem is that a harness is much more expensive than a collar, and as I'm sure you've noticed, puppies grow quickly, so the harness may not fit for long. When they are very small, you may be able to find budget brands to get you through the first 4 months. The main considerations are that it's soft, safe, and secure. Many of the cheaper puppy harnesses fit over the head – the problem here is that dogs can easily find this unpleasant, so you may need to be patient and make it fun.

Never force the harness over the puppy's head, you will be setting them up to find it more and more unpleasant, and they'll actively avoid it. The other consideration in regard to budget brands is that they may not be designed well enough to spread the dog's weight, and instead, the force is all in one place at the bottom of the dog's neck. It's worth the investment in quality, well-known, brands if possible. It's very tempting to attach the leash to the dog's collar. After all, it's cheaper, it's less hassle, and it's what we did for years, before the popularisation of the harness. But knowing what I know today, I will never again attach a leash to my dog's collar.

Why I don't walk dogs by their collar

If we could see inside the dog's neck, we'd see many vital structures. We'd see the oesophagus (food-pipe) and the trachea (windpipe) with the delicate epiglottis which shuts the trachea when swallowing. We all know that the tightening of anything around the neck causes a restriction of breathing and in extreme cases leads to death. The structure of a dog's neck is no different in this respect, they feel the same discomfort that we'd feel if we were to have a collar placed around the neck, a leash attached, and somebody pulling us around.

At the top of the neck sits a scaffold of tiny bones known as the hyoid apparatus – their job is to support the larynx, which, in turn, holds the vocal cords and helps with swallowing and breathing. Very close to the front surface of the neck (at about collar height) sits the thyroid cartilage and thyroid gland. The thyroid gland produces the hormones thyroxine and triiodothyronine, which affect how every cell in the body works. Unfortunately, the thyroid gland can't regenerate following damage. This fact alone, is a reminder that no mammal on earth evolved to withstand excessive pressure or impact to the front of the neck. Around the same area as the thyroid gland there are also parathyroid glands. The job of the parathyroid glands is to regulate calcium. Calcium regulation is more important than we might think – calcium regulation is crucial for many of the dogs' internal organs to function properly.

At the back of the neck the dog has seven cervical vertebrae which form the top of the spine. Interestingly, this is the same number in humans, giraffes, and almost all mammals (sloths and manatees are the only exceptions) – again, we're all aware of how vital the spine is and how painful and debilitating damage to it can be. Running the length of the cervical vertebrae is the nuchal ligament. This is the amazing piece of anatomy which allows the dog to have an outstretched head, or walk with the nose against the ground sniffing, with ease. It's not that the rest of the neck is super strong, it's that they have a substantial nuchal ligament taking the strain and working a little like the chains of a drawbridge. If you've ever given your dog a chew-treat called a paddywack (sometimes spelt paddywhack), then you've held in your hand the nuchal ligament of a sheep or bovine.

There are other vital components running through the neck within easy reach of damage, for example, the jugular vein and the vagus nerve; additionally, there are many conditions of the neck (for example, laryngeal paralysis and tracheal collapse) which, if not caused by, would certainly be exacerbated by neck pressure – and it's not only the neck; a study by Pauli (2006) found that collar pressure significantly increased intraocular pressure (pressure within the eyes). The study found no such effect when using a harness. A more recent study (Carter et al., 2020) tested various collar types and found all of them to carry significant risk of injury to dogs that pull, even at low forces – but I think the point has been made, that it's not a good idea to be applying pressure to the neck of our beloved dogs.

A concern I often hear about harnesses is that they teach dogs to pull. The reasoning behind this is that they've been used for years by sled dogs. The reason they're used on sled dogs is that it's the most ergonomic way to pull the sledge. Ergonomics relate to efficiency and comfort. It's fairly obvious that it wouldn't be efficient or comfortable to pull by the neck – but making the dog less comfortable (so less efficient at pulling) is not a reasonable argument against the use of a harness. I want my dogs to be as comfortable as possible; if we introduce elements of discomfort the dog will not be at ease or be in the best emotional state for training or generally interacting with the world. If the dog pulls, this is more reason to use a harness, not less reason.

The Home Environment

From a human perspective, we like our homes to be pee-free and the furniture to be unchewed, but what is a puppy to make of a brand new home? So many new smells to investigate and lovely, soft, absorbent rugs to pee on. Once the puppy gains a little confidence you can bet they will be investigating every nook and cranny. It's hard work watching a puppy and ensuring they don't damage our things or injure themselves. We tend to start off well, but we're easily distracted, especially with our smartphones being so easily to hand. The very simple way of making our lives a little easier and ensuring the puppy is as safe as possible is to set up the home accordingly. Put away anything which might easily be damaged, keep your shoes and handbags well out of reach, preferably in a cupboard or room the puppy doesn't have access to. It's not just the damage to your items that should concern you –

it's the harm it could cause to a puppy who chews or eats toxins.

A very common cause of poisoning in dogs is actually through the consumption of human medication. Consider how many harmful things are lurking in the average handbag or purse. Go around the house and ensure the puppy cannot gain access to any electrical cables or sockets. Pups have no way of understanding that rubbery cables have electricity running through them and that one bite could kill them. From the dog's point of view, it's something to be investigated, and they investigate everything with their mouths.

When you bring a puppy home, it's tempting to introduce them to the world, but really, introductions to the neighbour or your friends and relatives can wait. The first few days are about ensuring that this little bundle of joy feels safe. Keep things calm. I've seen so many videos over the years of young children being given a puppy as a surprise. Excited or emotionally overwhelmed children are not what the puppy needs – the pup will do best in an environment of calm stability.

Make introductions slowly, maybe one child at a time. Let the pup make choices of where they want to go, rather than being passed around like a game of pass the parcel. You might read this and think you have to get everything just right – you don't – but if we want to start off well, we really need to consider the dog's perspective. What is a tiny puppy, just removed from their mother, going to make of it all? Our number one priority is to let them feel safe.

I do not think our job is to rule over the dog like some kind of master who must be obeyed. This idea has ruined many millions of relationships. From a dog's point of view, what might it mean when we repeatedly insist they immediately do everything we ask? I'm not anti-training; I love training. I love building a relationship and working with the dog, but if we just expect dogs to blindly *obey*, we're missing the point. No animal on earth evolved to have all their decisions made for them. Can you imagine expecting any other animal to do the things we expect of dogs? If we attempted to train an ostrich, would we get angry if they failed to sit on command? Would we call the cat disobedient if they failed to come when called? No, we wouldn't. We'd understand that if we want these animals to do something, we'd better work out a way of convincing them it was their idea to do it. Instead of celebrating how utterly brilliant our dogs are we somehow just expect them to hand over all their free will to us. My aim is never to take their free will; my aim is to respect it, and employ it as I guide them through life.

I've been around for a long time, and I know only too well how words can be misunderstood so, for clarity, this does not mean we should let dogs do whatever they want. We have a responsibility to ensure their safety and the safety of others around them. We have a responsibility to ensure they are not a nuisance to other people or animals. We have a responsibility to ensure, as best we can, they are comfortable in their environment.

First Nights

Deciding where your new puppy should sleep is often a big dilemma. Traditional advice was to leave the puppy by themselves. The problem with this idea is that the pups will usually vocalise their distress throughout the night. This is somewhat problematic for the human because it may keep them awake or cause awkwardness with the neighbours, who didn't sign up for sleepless nights. However, from the pup's perspective, they've just been taken from their mother, from their littermates, and from everything that was familiar to them.

They've never been apart from their littermates or mum and now, the first time that happens, they're suddenly left alone. What else would they do but call out in distress? Why have we used this procedure for so long? We've continued to use it because it seems to work. By that, I mean the pup eventually stops crying out. We keep doing it because we think it works. I think we need to question this idea. Just because the puppy stops crying out doesn't mean they are no longer distressed or unhappy. It could equally (or more likely) be that the dog has simply given up on anybody coming to help. Imagine if you were locked inside a strange house; how long would you call for help before giving up? A few days? A few weeks? Eventually you would stop calling for help because it doesn't work. But that's not the point at which you'd suddenly become happy or content. You wouldn't suddenly be okay just because you'd given up calling, would you? We can easily fool ourselves into believing that an 8-week-old puppy is content just because they're not making a fuss – but personally, I can't see how that's likely to be true.

Ten years previously, I'd convinced myself that letting the dog cry it out was the right thing to do. My Labrador, Mr B., was my absolute pride and joy. He was a superstar of a dog. He made me smile just to look at him. He was my training dog throughout my canine behaviour degrees. He knew over 300 tricks and was fantastically well behaved. But as a puppy, Mr B. had been left in a crate downstairs. He went through about a week of vocalised distress at night-time. He developed into a great dog, so perhaps no long-term harm was done, but today I look back with great sadness for leaving him alone like that.

Before bringing Monty, my new puppy, home, I set up a large dog pen next to my bed. I could also have used a large crate, but I decided on a pen so that I could easily sit in there with him if needed. It's so close I can reach through the bars when I'm in bed. Inside is a soft dog bed, some toys, a heartbeat warming pillow (to replicate mum, to a very small degree), and a water bowl. On the first day, I introduced Monty to the pen, letting him have a sniff around (without closing the door) several times throughout the day. At night-time I placed him in the pen. I had a long fold out cushion prepared so I could lie beside the pen; however, when I placed him inside he settled on his bed without any distress, so I chose to lie in bed next to him and give him reassuring touches through the bars of the pen. I set the alarm for 2 AM to take him to the garden, but we will discuss this further in the section on toilet training. Monty slept very well (as he has done ever since) without showing any outward signs of distress. Please read the section on crates and pens as many dogs may not take to the crate/pen so readily.

All dogs are different, and some will inevitably be more distressed than Monty. They may need to be closer to you. Some people sleep with new puppies on/in their bed, but there's the obvious risk of them falling off the bed, and having dogs on your bed is a very personal choice. My first choice, if they need the extra support, would be to lie on the floor with them. Safety concerns should always take priority so you must ensure the puppy can't get into anything dangerous, for example, electrical cables, while you are sleeping. I find the sleeping pen to be the most practical way of achieving this.

Not everyone wants a dog in their bedroom. For most of my life with dogs, they never came into the bedroom. This changed for me about 5 years previously when I moved house. I knew the dogs were a little unsettled in the new environment, so I let them sleep in the bedroom – they seemed happier, and we never went back. Given the choice, I think many dogs would choose to sleep near to their humans, but if that's not something you want to allow, the separation can come later, when the puppy is a little older, maybe moving the pen a little further from you in small increments over time. Another option, if you don't want dogs in the bedroom, may be for you to sleep downstairs (or in whatever area they sleep in) for a little while. If you have other dogs, some puppies will quickly settle in to sleeping near them and the transition away from you may be a little easier.

Crates and Pens

Opinions about dog crates can often be polar opposite. During the research for this book, I came across two other authors who hold very opposing views. The first, recommended the use of crates, stating that it will eliminate any possibility of separation anxiety. The second author advised against the use of crates, claiming them to be harmful.

The rationale of the first author was that dogs will always feel safe in the crate so can't get anxious. The second author claimed that the dog is trapped in a crate so cannot feel safe. The rationale here seems to be that there are no doors on the dens of free-ranging pups and that safety requires the ability to leave at will.

So, who's correct?

I do not agree with either of these writers. Separation related distress is a complex problem which isn't fixed by simply confining the dog to a crate. If it were so easy, there would be no cases of separation distress. A crate may prevent the dog from damaging the house, but it is not a cure for the dog's anxiety, and in some cases will make it worse. Separation anxiety is exactly that; anxiety brought about by separation from their human guardians.

The second author (who was against the use of crates) gave a more logical argument. However, our puppies are not free-ranging dogs. They are under our care and it's for us to ensure they come to no harm. The argument against the use of doors could easily be extended to our homes. I don't think anyone is quite ready to remove their external doors to allow the dog a more natural existence. Additionally, free-ranging dogs have a very high mortality rate – approximately 80% do not survive past the age of 7 months (Paul et al., 2016).

It's not just these authors. There is a big divide amongst the dog training community regarding the use of crates. And arguing with passionate dog lovers is a tough gig. It's akin to trying to change somebody's religion or political allegiance. But what do I think? I don't think crates are appropriate for long-term use or for dogs to spend the day in with no opportunity to find other resting spots.

I don't think pups should be placed in there as an easy fix, as punishment, or to lock problems away. I *do* think that when pups are introduced to crates slowly, and with choice (not immediately locking them in, but allowing them to acclimatise and feel safe), they can be a great asset in keeping pups safe if we are unable to watch them for short periods. They allow the pup to sleep near us but remain safe while we sleep. A third reason for crate training is obvious too. If the dog ever needs to stay over at the vet or wait at the groomer's salon, it stands to reason that this stressful event will be made slightly easier if the dog has been crate trained previously. In an ideal world, we would be available to watch the puppy 24/7 and they'd never need to stay at the vets, but I must consider what's likely, not just what's ideal. Some countries have taken the decision to ban the use of crates, for example Sweden and Finland, except for transportation and medical recovery. I'm a little concerned about this approach because it may increase stress for dogs recovering in crates if they have not previously been acclimatised to them.

Crate/pen training

Crates and pens need to be introduced appropriately. If we simply place the puppy inside and shut the door, a great many puppies will become anxious. It is far better to give them plenty of opportunities to go in and out of the crate by themselves, perhaps having toys and food inside to make it the best experience possible. Crates need to have a cosy bed inside and they need a water bowl (one which can't be easily knocked over).

Allow the puppy to explore the crate in their own time. Perhaps leaving the door open for them to come and go as they wish. It's important to begin with that the puppy can come back out; this should prevent them feeling trapped or developing an instant fear or dislike of the crate/pen. Immediately closing the door may also work against what we are trying to achieve because, if the pup isn't happy about the enclosure, they are far less likely to want to go back inside. When they are happily going in and out and having naps inside, you can begin the process of shutting the door. Start with a half-closed door, then nearly closed, but open enough that they can push it open to come out.

Finally, you can lock the door, but don't lock it and walk away. At this stage its best to lock it and immediately unlock it again. You could practice by placing a few treats inside to keep the puppy occupied and enjoying the process. Gradually, you could lock the door for a little longer each time, before opening it again.

If the puppy is not enjoying it, we've done too much too quickly. In this case we should make things easier so they can enjoy it rather than the issue escalating into a long-term problem. We can go right back to the beginning if necessary, leaving the door open, then start again, but more slowly.

With crate/pen training there's an obvious problem. It could easily take days or weeks for the pup to become happily content to be inside with the door closed. This is a problem which never seems to be addressed in crate training protocols. However, with a new puppy, people often want or need (for safety reasons) them to be in there on the first night. Ideally, if you plan to use a crate/pen, it would be better to begin crate training while the puppy is with their breeder as this would make for a far easier transition. One solution may be to set up the crate in such a way that you can lie next to it for a few nights. As explained earlier, with my new puppy, I planned to sleep on a fold out foam mattress beside his pen; however, he settled down so well that it wasn't needed.

Life stages

Puppies seem to develop into adult dogs within the blink of an eye. Their life expectancy, of course, is much shorter than the average human life. However, just as humans go through various life stage transitions, so do our dogs.

It's astonishing, but the gestation period of dogs is just 63 days. 63 days to grow into a living breathing puppy dog. In comparison, the gestation period of a human is around 280 days and for an elephant it's an incredible 680 days.

From 0-2 weeks of age pups are within the neonatal stage. They are deaf (because the ear canals are not yet open) and blind, but they can already smell and taste. This aids their instinctive drive to find the mother's teat and drink. However, they are still highly vulnerable as they cannot yet regulate body temperature. At this very early stage of their lives they spend approximately ninety percent of their time sleeping. It's believed that handling them gently at this stage (gentle touches or holding them in your hands for a few seconds) helps them better cope with future stress.

Following the two-week neonatal period is the transitional period, which spans weeks 2 to 4. During this time, they develop their ability to hear, see, regulate body temperature and even begin wagging their tail. Their startle response develops, and brain activity dramatically increases.

We now move to some very important life stages known as the primary and the secondary socialisation periods. You may also note that the life stages now begin to overlap somewhat and are not absolute, but should be considered as a guide. The primary socialisation period of the dog covers from approximately week 3 to week 6. The puppy becomes very aware of their littermates and interacts with them socially. This period is thought to help pups develop bite inhibition, enabling them to develop fine motor control of their jaw and prevent biting too hard. When pups play-bite our hands (with our sensitive, furless, skin) it still hurts due to those very sharp baby canine teeth, but they are not usually applying much pressure.

It's sometimes stated that the lack of bite inhibition is the cause of serious bites on humans when the dog is older. One book I read, many years ago, claimed that a serious bite occurred after the dog had their tail shut in a car door. The author contended that this was caused by a lack of bite inhibition. I didn't believe it then, and I don't believe it now. Imagine, from the dog's perspective, the sudden and immense pain of their tail being slammed in a car door. Are we to believe that, had they developed bite inhibition as a pup, then they would have just given a gentle bite causing no harm? In that moment of absolute agony, they are likely to respond with every bit of force they can muster. I don't believe bite inhibition plays any significant role in a situation such as this. Bite inhibition may prevent accidental injury, for example, in play – it's not likely to prevent a dog from inflicting injury from a point of rage, or where they feel the need to bite hard. I certainly wouldn't feel safe next to any dog having their tail shut in a car door; bite inhibition or no bite inhibition. Nevertheless, having littermates seems to play an important role in the social skills of dogs. Those from single litters are at greater risk of finding it difficult interacting or playing with other dogs as they mature.

The secondary socialisation period covers approximately 5-12 weeks. This is often considered to be the most influential period of a dog's life. This is a period of time when they are likely to be more accepting of novel stimuli. However, from week 5, inquisitiveness is conflicting (to some degree) with fearfulness. At week 7 inquisitiveness and fearfulness are about even, but caution of novel things may begin to take over the will to investigate, and by week 12, introducing the puppy to new things may get slightly trickier. All animals have these critical periods of socialisation, but they are vastly different lengths. Dogs may have evolved from a wolf type animal but, through the process of domestication, their socialisation period has lengthened considerably. The wolf has a socialisation window of just three weeks. If they haven't had contact with humans within the first 3 weeks of life, they're likely to remain cautious of them their entire life. From an evolutionary perspective, socialisation periods allow animals to be at ease with the environment they're born into, whilst being cautious of novelty (things they didn't experience as an infant), because novelty could equal danger. It's obviously not possible for an infant to learn about every possible predator/danger – it's much simpler to just be cautious of the things you've not experienced before.

However, these are not absolute rules, and domestication and then the process of humans selectively breeding dogs for a multitude of purposes has undoubtedly had a big impact. For example, Labradors tend to be friendly towards strangers, whereas German Shepherds tend to be wary of strangers once the socialisation period is over. The problem is, of course, that our companion dogs don't tend to see much of the world before the socialisation period finishes because they must wait for vaccinations to be completed. I think it's generally a good idea to introduce them to the world they will live in as early as possible, but ensuring the experience is a pleasant one and done safely.

My puppy, Monty, will need to travel well in my car. From the time we brought him home he had about 3 weeks before he would be safely covered by his vaccinations, but each day I carried him to the car and let him have a sniff around inside of the car crate. We visited the office I work from (a few days a week), because he will be in the office too. We visited the main areas that I will walk him and we went in some elevators. To reduce risk I carried him, but these early experiences will make it easier for him to be at ease with elevators and the world around him as he grows.

There are some good arguments for introducing them to absolutely everything they might ever encounter, but that's quite a difficult task, and it might also become a little overwhelming and exhausting for the puppy. I think we should consider what's most important for our particular dog. For me, I really do want him to be able to use the elevator and travel in the car without anxiety. For others that wouldn't be a priority because they might never need to take their dog inside an elevator, and they may not drive. In such cases it may be wise to take them on a few buses and some rides in a friend's car or taxi. The priority is ensuring the puppy remains happy and finds the world around them pleasant, or at the very least, not scary.

Because the pup is steadily becoming fearful/cautious of new things during the period from 5-12 weeks of age, it is also known as the first fear response. Although the puppy needs to learn about the environments in which they will live, we must try to avoid the puppy becoming frightened at this time because during this highly influential time of brain development, frightening events, may cause the puppy to be anxious into and even throughout adulthood. This is a very good reason not to take a heavy-handed approach with puppies – it is not only their life that is being made more difficult due to bad experiences in puppyhood, it's also more difficult for the human to have the relaxed, easy-going, dog they want. Whatever we want from a dog, from companionship to agility champion, it will be more difficult to achieve with an anxious/fearful dog.

Between the ages of 12–16 weeks the puppy becomes more agile, gains confidence around the home, and learns that they can easily outmanoeuvre the human, who must feel rather slow to the dog. Teeth may now start to be replaced by the adult teeth – the ones we are really waiting to go are the four long canines towards the front, they are the ones making our hands sore during puppy play. But it could be around week 20 before they are finally ready to fall out.

At around 4 to 8 months is a stage known as the flight instinct. This is the puppy becoming more independent and they may wander a greater distance from us. We may also find that their recall begins to fail. They are more willing to explore the world, and this may seem more interesting than running back to their human when asked to do so. This is often seen as disobedience, but it really isn't. It's just an animal making what seems to be the right choices for themselves. This is something every animal, throughout the millions of years of evolution, has had to do. None of them evolved to be a slave to another species or have all their decisions made for them by humans. Even within their own species, all animals reach a time when they must be more independent. It may interfere with our training needs, but it's quite normal for dogs to develop selective hearing and begin to ignore us. Through training we can teach them that it really is a good idea to come back to their human when called, but we shouldn't expect them to magically think that returning to the human is more important than chasing other dogs and having a great time. Why would they think that? I actually think that teaching a fantastic recall is relatively straight forward, but humans often make an absolute hash of it by being bossy or reprimanding the dog when he eventually returns. What we then get is a slower and slower return. It's like we are determined to make life as difficult as possible. If you want a fabulous recall, please ensure you read the recall chapter in this book. It may be the most valuable thing you ever teach the dog.

Adolescence occurs between the ages of 5-14 months. The dog becomes stronger, faster, and skilful in their movement. The dog may appear fully formed but care should be taken not to overwork their ligaments, tendons and joints, which may not yet be fully formed or strengthened. The brain reaches full functionality, and the dog is capable of learning complex tasks. Males may start lifting their leg to scent mark and females will begin their oestrous cycles. Reproductive hormones may lead to some difficulties in training, especially in the dog's ability to concentrate on specific tasks. This is just one of the reasons that training works best when spread over many short sessions, rather than expecting the dog to focus on us for an hour or more. I've trained many behaviours over the years, but mostly, they have been built up by doing just a few minutes, several times per day.

During the adolescence period (5-14 months), and possibly connected to the rise of reproduction hormones, there is also a second fear response stage. Dogs are susceptible to regressing into fearfulness and anxiety, especially if socialisation has been lacking. Adulthood begins between 2 to 4 years of age. Females tend to mature at a younger age than males, and small breeds tend to mature earlier than large breeds. The work we've done in helping the puppy develop may now stand them in good stead throughout life.

From 7 years onwards the dog begins to slow down – this is the geriatric stage. They are at greater risk of developing cognitive decline and arthritic conditions. However, they are more than capable of continuing to enjoy life in a loving and caring home.

Body language

A puppy's body language is a rich source of information, yet this valuable source of information often goes unnoticed. However, once we start looking for it, it's difficult not to see. If we don't notice the dog is fearful or stressed, further problems may develop. For example, after a family dog bites somebody, the family may feel that the dog bit without warning. I don't claim it is impossible, but I do think it's improbable.

The signs are usually there, we just fail to take notice and help the dog cope or ensure safety. Too often we are sure the dog would never bite. It's not likely to be their first option. If it was, I doubt humans would have formed such a close and enduring relationship with them. However, we should never assume it will not happen. Any dog can be pushed (often inadvertently) to bite. Don't just be a person with a puppy – be a puppy watcher. Notice their behaviour, their posture, their gaze, how they move, their likes, and dislikes. It's fascinating, and it's often silent.

Silence is something which I really love about the animal world. Animals are often vocal, but not in the same way as humans. I prefer body language; body language is usually how I recognise people. I have prosopagnosia (face blindness), so I'm terrible at recognising faces. I recognise movement and a person's (or animal's) gait almost instantly. I could sit and watch animals all day, every day, but that wouldn't get this book written.

Stretching, Scratching, and Sniffing

Stretching, scratching, and sniffing are all examples of displacement behaviours. Displacement behaviours are those which are performed outside of their usual context and when the dog is feeling conflicted or unsure. But how do we know if scratching is a displacement behaviour or just occurring because the dog has an itch? If they begin to scratch the moment they're taken into a training class, or there's another sudden change of environment, we can make a good guess that the behaviour is displacement. The dog is most likely excited by all the other dogs but equally unsure or nervous. Ideally, they'd probably prefer fewer dogs in the class or a greater distance to watch them from. Dogs also perform stretching as a calm greeting gesture, often reserved for people they are particularly fond of.

Yawning, Looking Away, Tongue Flicks, and Lip Licking

These all indicate that the puppy is stressed and uncomfortable with something. Turning away is often an attempt to disengage, just as we might look away when people stand too close to us. Tongue flicks are common and are a good indicator that the dog is feeling uncomfortable and pressured. By watching my puppy Monty, I was able to spot there was something he doesn't like about getting into the back of my car. From approximately 4 months of age, he would place his front paws up and I'd help him in. As he grew taller, he began to, mostly, jump in by himself. He was usually keen because I always placed a few treats inside. At six months of age his behaviour changed; rather than jump straight in, he would look around in every direction other than the car. Sometimes dogs are just looking around, but the pattern of behaviour told me something was wrong. In the car was a large dog crate, made specifically for the car; as I was looking for a possible cause to Monty not wanting to jump in, I realised he had grown so large he could no longer stand in the crate and lift his head up in a natural position. Even sitting, his head touched the roof of the crate. I removed the crate and within two days he was back to jumping into the car without any issues. Sometimes it is difficult to spot the cause of the problem. For example, dogs may be suffering from joint pain or an undiagnosed injury, so if you can't see a reason for behaviour change you should get the dog examined by a veterinarian. We're often keen to tell dogs what to do, but we also need to take a step back and consider what the dog is telling us.

Eyes

Dilated pupils (also known as mydriasis) are an indicator of arousal and may be seen at times of alarm, when the body is preparing for the fight-or-flight response. Dilation also occurs during joyful arousal, for example, when greeting family members. A hard-fixed stare often signals a threat in the animal world; with this in mind, it's probably not such a good idea to stare into the dog's eyes to see if they're dilated or not. Far more noticeable than pupil dilation is when the dog shows the white (sclera) of their eyes. This is known as whale eye and is caused when the dog looks at something intently without moving their head in the same direction. Whale eye (often seen during resource guarding) often indicates intense stress which could be followed by a snap or bite. Sadly, I've seen this expression in many online photos where small children or babies are too close, clambering over, pulling at or sitting on the dog. These photos are often an attempt to show the world just how wonderful the dog is with the child, but to anyone well-versed in dog body language they are a catastrophe waiting to happen. The dog may tolerate such stress without ever snapping but we can never know the dog's tolerance level (which is fluid rather than fixed) until it's too late and disaster happens. If there is one thing we can all do to prevent dog bites, it is to understand that dogs are not okay with things just because we think they should be; they need us to look out for signals of distress and give them the space they need.

Mouth

An active but happy and relaxed dog usually has an open mouth and very relaxed lower jaw. A tightly closed mouth may indicate that the dog is more tense and vigilant. Lip curling to display the teeth is usually interpreted as a threat signal. This doesn't necessarily mean that the dog actively wants to fight; more likely it indicates that they want the other dog, person, or whatever they see as a threat, to go away. But it could easily escalate to serious aggression if not handled correctly. The dog may need to be given more space to prevent escalation.

Ears

Holding ears in a backwards direction may be a sign of fear or appeasement (demonstrating they are no threat in order to de-escalate perceived tension). Erect, or lifted ears indicate that the dog is alert. However, there are so many different ear types that it's important to get to know your own dog's ears when they're relaxed, fearful or alert. If ears ever played a role in dog-to-dog body language, artificial selection for particular ear types has almost certainly restricted this ability.

Raised Paw

A raised front paw may indicate the dog is apprehensive. They also do this when puzzled by something or in anticipation of what's about to occur. This behaviour is utilised in pointing dogs (specialised hunting dogs) who remain stationary, pointing towards the scent of prey with one leg raised. This traditionally gave hunters the time to prepare before the prey was spooked. Rather than simply seeing a cute behaviour, puppy guardians should think about what the pup may be concerned about.

Shake-Off

The dry shake-off looks very similar to the shake-off that dogs perform after getting wet but as the name suggests it's done when dry. This is often performed following a play session with another dog, or sometimes a human, and is thought to be a mechanism for calming down after all the excitement. You may also see it following other stressful or exciting events.

Low Body Posture

Low body posture usually indicates fear and appeasement. The dog is communicating that they are no threat. This shouldn't be taken to mean that they will not bite, only that they are fearful and don't want to fight; however, if their discomfort is ignored the dog could still become aggressive out of desperation. The body language that many people interpret as the guilty look (head and body held low with slow conflicted movements) when the dog has been 'naughty' is actually an appeasement gesture.

This often occurs when the guardian returns home to find that the dog has been in the kitchen bin and scattered trash all over the floor, or some other minor disaster. But this is not guilt; the dog has learned to associate the bin being knocked over with an angry human, so they become anxious. They cannot assess their earlier behaviour as 'naughty' and feel guilty about it, but they have the outstanding ability to associate knocked over bins with angry humans.

Tail

It is usually assumed that a wagging tail means the dog is happy. This may be true, but it depends how the tail is wagging. Tails which are raised are often an indicator of an aroused, alert or agitated state. A wagging tail held high, especially arching over the back may be a threat display, and slow wags may indicate that the dog is unsure. A low tucked tail often indicates fear. However, dogs may also tuck their tail when they're concentrating, for example, when they have a food dispensing enrichment toy.

Happy dogs often wag their tail in a circular motion and sometimes, when excited and happy, their hips join in with the wag and they seem to wag with half of their body. But we must also take the breed type into consideration; different breeds may have different positions in which they naturally hold the tail.

Greyhounds have a very low tail position whilst beagles tend to naturally hold their tails high. Others, such as the bulldog, have a short (usually curled) tail. Just as with ears, humans have altered the dogs' conspecific (dog-to-dog) communication repertoire.

We should evaluate body language in relation to everything else that's going on around the pup (the environment); what's the puppy telling us? As a means of telling us how they're feeling, body language is all they have; don't ignore it, use it to help them, and use it to help your relationship.

Attention Seeking

So you have an attention seeker! What does this mean? Attention seeking is a concept. It is something we've constructed in our minds to explain the dog's behaviour. But what's really going on? When the pup was initiating play with his littermates, nobody called that attention seeking. What we should be saying is he wants to play, he's initiating interaction, he's building relationships and bonds. Dogs are incredibly social beings and connection is vitally important to that.

When I was much younger, I was told, by the trainers of the day, that you should never let the dog initiate interaction with you. This, it was thought, would signal to the dog that they are in charge. Today, we know this idea is plain wrong. The dog's brain is remarkably similar to our own. The biggest difference is in its size. An average dog brain is the size of a lemon; the human brain is about the size of a cantaloupe melon. The human also has a much larger cortex and more folds, and the frontal lobes are bigger. However, our olfactory bulbs are tiny compared to those of the dog. But the brain of man and dog are similar in many respects. Both have the caudate nucleus, tightly packed with dopaminergic receptors, closely related to reward, learning, and motivation. As discussed in the introduction to this book, we also share the same primary emotional circuits, identified by Jaak Panksepp. We have different specialisations; people are not dogs and dogs are not people, but fundamentally, we are not quite as different as people often assume.

Dogs, like people, have emotional and social needs and as dogs are captive (not free to do as they please or fulfil their own needs) it falls on us, as their carer, to do all we can to ensure those needs are met. When the puppy chooses to interact I think it's a wonderful moment of connection between two separate species. It is, in my opinion, the closest connection we have with another species and it's extremely special. There are two things I really love about having dogs. The first is simply walking with them in a quiet place, just me and them – no pressures, no instructions, just walking in a nice place, looking at the beauty of nature and watching the dog wander and sniff; both of us at peace with the world. The second thing is the special connection which doesn't need words or explanations. When I'm feeling low, the dog doesn't ask questions; I don't have to explain anything; I just feel the connection between us with no pressure to be or do or say anything at all.

There are, of course, difficult times. There are times when we are tired, when we've had a hard day, and pups being pups, want to connect by jumping all over us and running zoomies around the living room or use our hands as a chew toy. I was contacted recently about this very problem. The lady's pup was well behaved all day but would become very active in the evening for a few hours and in her words, was 'extremely naughty.' This was interesting because Monty was also becoming very excited for a few hours each evening. These times with a puppy can be challenging, but it's important that we don't let our frustration take over.

When pups are getting over-aroused, we often try to control this by telling them to calm down, or telling them to stop it. What does this mean to an excited puppy? It doesn't address their needs in any way. It's like saying *'don't bother me with your aroused, excited, tired, immature brain, I'm not interested.'*

Many people with this problem try to tire the puppy out; however, playing exciting games, such as fetch, may increase arousal and doesn't actually induce the brain into a calmer state. My preferred options to help Monty when he becomes over excited/aroused in the evening is to put his leash on and take him outside to sniff around. I don't walk any further than I need to, I just spend 15 minutes letting him sniff – this isn't suitable for everyone though, it depends on your location because it needs to be reasonably quiet, which in the evening, my area is.

Sniffing the scents of the outside world usually works well for shifting the brain out of that over excited state. The other thing I do, is that I always have a good supply of long-lasting chew items – see chapter on chewing. Beef tendons and lamb's feet seem to be the better items at the moment. Even if nothing else, this gives you a break from the growing puppy jumping on you and it prevents us getting into a situation where we are getting frustrated with them, which in the end, doesn't help them or us.

Sometimes it's Hard!

Having a puppy isn't all waggy tails and puppy cuddles - it can be hard work - it can be frustrating - it can be tiring - it can be cleaning pee out of your best rug - it can be sore hands from needle-sharp teeth - it can be chewed furniture, despite having a thousand toys - it can be standing in the freezing cold waiting for them to go to the toilet at 3 AM - it can be an overexcited puppy doing zoomies around the living room and launching themselves at you, it can be frustrating and tiring and exasperating. It's usually worth it in the end, but the early days can sometimes be overwhelming for the human. Nobody ever warns us about this, and it may be difficult to talk about. We might feel silly getting upset! After all, puppies are supposed to be fun, right? The first thing to do is to recognise that other people feel the same; other people have been through these experiences. You are not an oddball for feeling overwhelmed and the pup is probably not abnormal either; although, sometimes it can easily feel that way.

Set your environment up in ways that will make life as easy as possible. For example, if they are getting into the trash, place the bins out of reach, and out of sight, if possible; always provide alternative activities or the little pupster will find their own. When things feel like they are going wrong or becoming too much, I like to ask myself a question. The question comes from a Buddhist teacher I once knew. I use this question for minor problems, and I also use it for the greatest of life's challenges. The question is simply this: *How can*

I best respond? Obviously, such a simple little question that we ask ourselves isn't going to guide us through life worry-free, but I find it a great help. When I ask myself *how can I best respond?,* I often don't have an obvious answer. It's difficult, if not impossible, to always know what the best response could be to any given situation. However, by asking *how can I best respond?,* it often becomes very clear how I definitely should not respond. It shines a light on our, often, kneejerk reaction to things. For example, imagine the dog is pulling hard on the leash. Imagine they yank forward. You bring them back to you by offering a treat, but they grab it and pull forward again. They pull you towards the road, then towards another dog, then towards some food which has been dropped on the pavement. It's really easy for us humans to lose our cool and act out of frustration – maybe yanking the dog backwards with force and yelling at them. But, deep down inside, that's not us, it's not how we want to behave, and it's certainly not teaching the dog much – other than informing them that we can sometimes be erratic. If we ask ourselves *how can I best respond?* then it's instantly obvious that *frustrated aggression* is most definitely not the way to go.

Consider the relationship

Animals prefer calm humans. With a calm human, they can feel safe. Volatile, unpredictable people may cause anxiety in dogs and anxiety isn't conducive to a good learning environment. When we're training, especially a new behaviour, it's really easy to become frustrated; we might not get the exact behaviour that we were hoping for; we might not even get close or we might think the dog knows it, only to find he suddenly doesn't. We might feel let down or a little embarrassed.

Reacting to our disappointment by reprimanding the dog (yanking, giving a harsh 'NO' or showing frustration in other ways) is the exact opposite of what is needed because the dog may become anxious, either right away or next time they are put in a similar situation; this makes the job of getting the behaviour we want more difficult and prevents the dog from enjoying the process.

We have to live with the fact that we are human, and it's extremely difficult to never show frustration, even if we know the problems it can cause. However, recognising that we slipped up is a good thing, it's a very good thing. It's what allows us to learn. If we don't recognise the frustration or the fact that it might be counterproductive then how can we ever improve?

What's the alternative? What should we do if the pup isn't behaving as we expected? We can treat it as information. The dog is doing a great thing; he is showing us that in this situation he may sometimes respond in this way. It's just information, and we get to enjoy working on changing how he feels and responds.

The puppy is not a machine; they're a living being with feelings, emotions, likes, and dislikes. If we recognise that we are experiencing frustration or acting in a way we don't like then we can take a break, think about it when we're in a calmer state and try again another time.

How many times do we hear dogs called stupid when, in fact, in the cold light of day we might better understand that the error is more likely to be ours. Maybe we asked too much, didn't recognise the dog's stress, or didn't recognise something in the environment affecting the dog.

We can say to ourselves, 'wow, I wasn't expecting that behaviour', and ask the question, *how can I best respond?* I'm pretty sure your answer will not be, 'with frustration.' It's actually a great opportunity to think about how to deal with such situations in future.

Whatever you're doing with the puppy, is it worth the stress? What's the worst that's going to happen if you're not successful today? Wouldn't you prefer a happy dog who feels safe and trusts you not to be reactive and unpredictable? At times of frustration it is best to guide the puppy onto something easier and end on a good note; take a break and return to the original task another day if you want to.

It's not always easy, but just being aware that it's often not an easy ride, filled with puppy kisses, is a good starting point to not becoming overwhelmed. With over 30 years of experience, three degrees in dog and animal behaviour, and now writing my third book, I still have some moments of puppy madness, when my new puppy, Monty, is a little hyper. Yesterday, I very nearly lost the food off my plate to a very springy puppy who seems to have rocket boosters where his legs should be. Don't believe everything is easy, it's often not, but our attitude can go a long way to altering our experience.

Raising a puppy is a journey, and no journey worth having is without a few bumps in the road. Recently, during an informal training session in my garden, Monty became very excited and began doing zoomies, which is basically running around as fast as possible in absolute joy. I attempted to do a hand target (an exercise where he touches the palm of my hand with his nose) to try and bring him back to a calmer state. Instead of the hand target he launched himself at my hand at full speed, mouth open, and nearly took my hand with him as he zoomed past. How could I best respond? I looked to the skies and let out a chuckle. Sometimes it goes wrong and we mess up, but so what? Seeing the funny side is far better than getting mad. It was my mistake, and not one I'll be making again in a hurry.

How dogs learn

There are many methods used in the world of dog training. For example, my book, *Dog Training & Behaviour: a guide for everyone,* lists and explains 23 different training methods. The common denominator of all these training techniques is association. Dogs learn through association. The associations they make influence how they feel about things. This is how relationships are made. This is why it is so important to build positive associations.

Take a moment to consider why your puppy comes running towards you when you call their name. Within the puppy's home, people don't usually struggle too much with this exercise. Outside can be a little more challenging, and we'll discuss this later, but at home the puppy will usually come running when you call. They even do this without much specific training, but why do they? They do it because when we get a puppy, we are usually excited to have them; we're in a good mood, we're happy when we call, and we might play a game, or give them food. They very quickly associate us calling them, with something pleasant. Many people have the idea that humans give commands and dogs obey, or sometimes do not obey. But from the pup's perspective somebody calling their name, especially someone they know and have a good relationship with, is just a signal. It's a signal that something good/fun/exciting is happening, or about to happen, and they run over to join in. Now consider what happens if we call the pup's name and then, as they run over to us, we yell at them, or we bop them on the nose when they arrive. What associations are we building here? We're building bad associations. We're causing the dog to associate his name being called, with unpleasant experiences. Through good associations, the dog learns that certain behaviours are worth doing, so they do them more often. Through bad associations, the dog learns that doing the behaviour leads to unpleasant consequences, so they are less likely to do the behaviour.

For this reason, people have often used unpleasant consequences in an attempt to teach dogs not to do particular behaviours; for example, using prong collars or shock collars to prevent dogs lunging at other dogs. There are growing ethical concerns about these methods and shock and prong collars are now banned in many countries, but leaving ethics to one side for a moment, there are some major problems with teaching dogs through unpleasant consequences, or aversives, as they are more accurately known in the world of behaviour and training.

Using aversives might teach the dog what not to do (technically it is suppressing behaviour) through the formation of negative associations, but there's a very big, and I mean humongous, problem. What associations are the dogs making? Is it only the association we intended? For example, perhaps the human wanted to stop the dog from barking at cyclists – each time the dog barked at a cyclist, the human pressed the remote control, thereby giving the dog an electronic shock to the neck, via the shock collar. It doesn't have to be a shock collar; the same principle applies to any aversive (unpleasant) event. The human is attempting to teach the dog not to bark at cyclists by associating the behaviour with an unpleasant event. For this to work, the dog needs to associate barking at cyclists, with the unpleasant event (the shock). But what other associations are possible? Perhaps the dog makes an association between barking (in general) and the aversive. You might think, so what? I don't like them barking, but from the dog's perspective, at any future time that they may feel the need to bark, they may experience some degree of anxiety (because of the bad association) stopping them expressing themselves; they may also become unpredictable due to fear. They may associate the shock with cyclists, causing them to fear cyclists or bicycles, because they now believe them to be painful.

Imagine how this could pan out at some future date when a small child approaches, pushing their bicycle along. It could result in really serious aggression, which seems out of character and out of nowhere. The dog could also associate the shock with the area they were in at the time, again, possibly resulting in anxiety, fear, or aggression in that location at a future date. They could associate it with being on-leash with their guardian, or with an unknown noise they heard just before the shock occurred. The list of possible unwanted associations could run into the hundreds. There are people who do not agree with me on this. There are people who use a lot of aversive training techniques. I simply say this: if we can train without them, why would we ever use them? Why would we risk the devastating consequences?

In addition to ethical issues and unintended side effects of aversive training, there's yet another thing to consider. It may teach the dog to avoid doing a particular behaviour, but it doesn't teach them what you want them to do instead, and it doesn't fix the dog's problem. Let's revisit our example of a dog who barks at cyclists. What reason might they have to bark at cyclists? There are various possible answers. Perhaps they fear bicycles, or have frustration at not being able to give chase, but whatever the reason - is creating an aversive association likely to make the dog feel better about cyclists? From the dog's perspective, she sees a cyclist, which probably causes some degree of anxiety, and they then receive an unpleasant event (shock or other aversive). The aversive may (or may not) prevent future barking, but it does nothing to make her feel better about cyclists; quite the opposite is likely. It doesn't help her cope with the environment, it makes coping more difficult. When we use aversive, punishment based, methods, we are failing to understand the dog's perspective. We may be altering the symptom, but we are not addressing the root cause.

People often get themselves into a way of thinking that concentrates on unwanted behaviours, or what we might consider bad or naughty behaviour. From the dog's perspective, the behaviours are not bad or naughty. From their perspective they are simply doing what seems appropriate to them. Consider the puppy who chews your shoe. They have a natural urge to chew, and a shoe makes a great chew toy; why wouldn't they chew it? Chewing the shoe has no connection with being naughty from the pup's perspective of life. Humans name it as a bad behaviour simply because it is not what we wanted, and now we've to go to the bother and expense of buying new shoes. It's somewhat ironic that humans often expect the dog to understand our perspective of how they should behave, yet we often fail, catastrophically, to understand the dog's perspective. It is not enough to only think about what behaviour we don't want. If we are to be considerate of the dog, we must also consider what behaviour we want them to do instead of the unwanted behaviour; this way, we at least have something we can work towards and something we can reward. We must also consider the dog's emotional needs. People often ask me how to train a particular behaviour; however, there's much more to training than the procedural steps of the behaviour you wish to develop. Being kind to the dog is the first step. Kindness is the first step to doing anything with the dog. It's the first step to a happy dog and a happy dog is much easier to train. Every behaviour I can think of is more easily and more pleasantly trained when there is already a good relationship in place.

It's easy to notice problem behaviour, because it causes us a problem. Very often problem behaviour isn't a problem for the dog at all, it's a problem for the human. We take notice of things that are problematic for us, but the real problem is that we don't notice the hundreds of behaviours the dog does each day which are not problematic. We don't notice, because they are not the behaviours of concern. However, if we take time to notice all the things the puppy does that we like and take the time to make those things rewarding, with a treat, a game, or just a little attention, we will get more of them.

Capturing & Default Behaviour

There is a method of training which is often underutilised. This method is known as capturing. Capturing is often under-used as a training method because it's not so useful for teaching particular behaviours in a particular time period. But it has a superpower. The most common error in dog training is that we reinforce behaviour only when we're purposefully training. But what about the rest of the time? Dogs don't just stop learning the moment a training session is over; dogs are always learning what pays and what doesn't. Humans learn a lot when they're not in the classroom; this is no different for dogs.

We are primed to notice behaviours we don't like; for example, barking at the postman or stealing food from the kitchen counter. But we often forget about the vast amount of time when the dog is not doing these things. Capturing can be used to reinforce the dog's behaviour choices at other times.

I call this 'default training' because it doesn't require any formal cues or requests from us. We can simply reinforce all the behaviours we like. In this way, we get more of these behaviours by default and simultaneously improve the dog/human relationship through pleasant associations.

Keep a little of the dog's daily food allowance, or perhaps a few treats, to one side in a container. If it's dry food, then it is handy to keep some in your pocket. Try to use this food each day for capturing behaviour which you like. For example, looking at you without barking when they hear a noise, lying quietly by your feet or on their bed, chewing their toys rather than the leg of your chair, standing back from the doorway as you open the door or resting their head on your lap. It doesn't need to be complex. To reinforce behaviour you like or appreciate; simply say 'yes' and give the reward (reinforcer). We then get more of these behaviours because they're what we're reinforcing. This isn't only good for the dog, it's good for us too. It teaches us to look out for the good stuff and see the dog from a more positive perspective. From the dog's perspective 'capturing' is a pleasant, stress-free, way to learn. There are no demands on them; they are just going about their business and every now and then they're getting a free treat – who wouldn't like that?

Note: if you are using some of the dog's daily food allowance for default training, you should ensure any that's left over is still given to the dog in other ways. The amount of food they get each day should not depend on their behaviour, but on their dietary requirements.

Toilet Training

Let's face it, nobody wants pee and poop in their home and us humans can become pretty stressed if the puppy toilets indoors. We can often expect too much from young puppies, but we really need to give them a break – compared to humans, who take years to develop full control of their bladder, dogs are pretty amazing, and if we set them up for success, by 12 weeks they can be fully house-trained. For others, it can take a little longer, but it really is on us humans to set things up right and to keep up our end of the deal.

The very first thing I do when a new puppy arrives is take them to the garden so they have the opportunity to toilet in the right place. Young pups need to pee and poop quite a lot so if we want to avoid accidents, we need to be giving them every opportunity to eliminate in the garden. My recommendation is that they are taken to the garden at least every 30 minutes for the first few weeks. This may sound excessive, but its only during the puppy's awake/active times and pups need a lot of rest/sleep, so it's not nearly as much as you might first think. Additionally, the times they are more likely to go to the toilet are after playing (or any excitement/stimulation), eating, drinking, and waking up. We should also be watching them the whole time. Circling, sniffing, whining, and scratching the ground or door, are all possible indicators that they may need to eliminate. Don't wait and see. Waiting to see is just giving an opportunity for them to toilet inside. If we want them to be amazing, and not toilet inside, then we must be amazing in our abilities to watch them and help them. After the first few weeks of being on high alert, things may become a little easier. You will, if you watch for it, learn their habits and behaviour patterns. You will notice how often they're going and how they suddenly change behaviour just before elimination. At this point you can begin to extend the time between garden visits, and you may notice them instinctively walking to the door (or looking at it) when they want to go outside.

Setting things up in ways which will make life easier on us is crucial to success. My home-office is upstairs. That makes it sound grand, but it's actually just a desk in a bedroom. It's quite a long way from the door to the garden. In fact, it's a flight of stairs and three doors away. That desk is where I usually work from (when working from home) and it's where I usually sit and write, or do webinars etc. But it wouldn't be such a good place for me to sit while house-training the new puppy. I've made my life easier by setting up a temporary desk (it's actually an old free-standing breakfast bar I had in the shed) in my kitchen. Now I'm right by the back door (to the garden). I've also placed a child gate on the kitchen door. I can now sit and work in the kitchen whilst also keeping a very good watch on Monty, and it's very easy to take him to the garden. We all have different situations and environments (and dogs) but it's about doing whatever we can to make it easier, not just for the dog but also for ourselves.

Another option may be to use puppy pads indoors for the puppy to eliminate on. It's not something I would choose in my situation but for many people in apartments, with no garden access, it can be useful and save lots of stress. Puppy pads work mainly because they are very absorbent, and dogs have an instinct to pee on absorbent surfaces. This is why most would prefer grass, rather than concrete. A good place for a puppy pad would be where it is obviously the most absorbent material, for example on a tiled floor. If your puppy is regularly using puppy pads you may move them steadily closer to the outside door. This way the puppy learns to go to the door, and you get the opportunity to take them outside.

Many pups may need to go to the toilet overnight, so if you really want to make the best of starts, set your alarm clock so you can take them out during the night. With Monty, I set the alarm for 2 AM and then 6am. However, he was quite sleepy at 2 AM and wasn't all that interested in going outside. I would place him on the kitchen floor while I unlocked the back door, but he would just wander to his bed (in the kitchen) and lay down. On the third night (9.5 weeks of age) I decided to take a chance, so I didn't set the 2 AM alarm. He slept right through the night and I took him out at 6 AM. I wasn't expecting him to be able to do this and many others will not be able to – we must remember that our dogs are individuals and have individual needs.

However, we must be realistic. If we get a young puppy, the chances are we are going to end up with a few accidents – responding to this in the right way is vital. In times gone by we were instructed to do all manner of ghastly things in order to teach dogs not to pee indoors. These very outdated ideas included wiping the pup's nose in the urine (or even faeces), hitting them on the nose, shouting 'no', throwing keys, or punishing the dog in some other way. We now know that, not only are these methods unkind and damaging to the human/animal bond, but they also do not work as intended. It's very likely that the dog would become fearful of going to the toilet when people are around. It doesn't necessarily teach them not to toilet in the house, but to only do it out of sight of people. From the dog's point of view, being reprimanded for going to the toilet must be extremely bewildering. They go from having the joyful new puppy guardians doting over them and rejoicing in their puppy antics, to being assaulted by those same people.

They have lost their littermates and the security of their mother; they're building a brand new relationship, a brand new life, with people they don't yet know all that well and BOOM, they're attacked as they relieve themselves. The human doesn't think it's an attack or an assault – they're just doing what they think they need to do; either that or they know better but are frustrated. The puppy has absolutely no way of understanding the human's motives – they are just confused and scared. This isn't just a nightmare for the dog, it's a nightmare for the human too because the dog is now more likely to hide before toileting, for example behind the sofa, and they are less likely to go when the human takes them outside, because they're now anxious with that human around them, especially when they get the urge to go to the toilet. What a mess. The dog gets bewildered, and the human makes it more difficult to get what they wanted – a house trained dog.

If you see the puppy going to the toilet inside the house, quietly and calmly pick them up and carry them to the garden; put them down, and let them finish their business. Then go and clean up the mess. There are lots of cleaning products on the market specifically designed for the job.

House-training can sometimes feel really stressful, but it doesn't have to be. The vast majority of dogs would choose to toilet outside given the opportunity; our job is to be good at facilitating that. This is quite amazing really, considering that dogs really didn't evolve to live inside our homes – we shouldn't be cross when they get it wrong, we should be amazed at their ability to, so often, get it right.

Some dogs do take a little longer than others. I see this more commonly in some of the toy breeds. It could be that they are so small it's more difficult for us to notice them begin to crouch, or maybe the small amount of pee is easier to go unnoticed (so not cleaned). Perhaps they are less tolerant of the cold wind or rain. If you have a small breed and are having difficulty, I recommend trying toilet training pads. They might not be ideal, but they are far better than the alternative of the dog peeing on your carpets. It would also be advisable to get a health check done by your veterinarian to rule out any medical problems.

Puppy Biting/Mouthing

Puppy biting can be one of the most frustrating things about caring for a puppy. Over the years, I've known it to bring many new puppy parents to tears. Many others have mistakenly labelled the pup as aggressive. In actual fact, puppy biting/mouthing is a very normal part of puppy development. Traditional advice was usually to squeal or yelp loudly so that the pup knows they've bitten too hard. This, however, doesn't usually work. The puppy could interpret the yelp as a chastisement and become fearful of you, or, and more likely, the yelp further stimulates the puppy to intensify the play biting. Putting the puppy in their crate is also not likely to help in the long term. It may give you a break from those sharp teeth but it means using the crate as a form of punishment, and this should never happen – the crate isn't somewhere you want the dog to feel stressed or frustrated because this prevents it being a nice place to hang out. It could very easily create anxiety whenever the dog needs to be in there, and this then makes it harder for us to have the dog relax in there. Additionally, removing the dog may prevent normal puppy development by preventing them from learning to control those teeth.

As I write this, Monty has just turned 12 weeks old and he's most active in the morning and evening. This is quite normal because dogs are crepuscular by nature (most active at dawn and dusk). This is when he seems to be really energised and needs to play the most. Each morning after he's been out to the toilet, I sit on the floor with him and we play. It's a beautiful one-to-one time. With our modern, busy, lives it can be difficult, but it's important to ensure you give the puppy some one-to-one time with you. Just you and them – forget about the rest of the world for a moment and put your phone away. A few weeks previously, Monty had five littermates to play with, now it's my job to be a playmate. Ignoring the puppy's needs is likely to result in an unhappy pup and a damaged house as they seek out stimulation wherever they can find it. However, there's no escaping the fact that playing with puppies of a certain age (approximately 9-18 weeks) can result in very sore hands from those pin-sharp puppy teeth. The vast majority of dogs will grow out of this, and in any case, they will be losing those sharp puppy teeth from about 16 weeks onwards. The sharp canines (these are the four longer teeth) usually get replaced at about 5 months of age.

Considering the difficulty we humans have with those sharp teeth against our sensitive thin skin, a backup plan is definitely required. My method is usually one of distraction. I make sure I have an abundance of toys that Monty can interact with. As is quite normal with pups, his attention span is relatively short and he goes from one toy to the next as I bring them alive by dragging them along, squeaking them, and throwing them. If he gets too mouthy and keeps catching my hands, I use two large soft toys (bigger than my hands) to play with him. Because the toys are bigger than my hands it's now difficult for him to make contact with my skin, but we still get to play, and he still gets great value from our interactions. I also like to use small sofa cushions/pillows for this game. Just a week before writing this part of the book, I posted this tip online. A few people were concerned that this would cause Monty to chew all other cushions and that I was teaching him bad habits. However, dogs are very good at learning context (so they get to know when we are playing the game) and also extremely good (much better than humans) at differentiating between objects.

If you find this difficult to believe, set up an experiment, throwing the dog's ball, one that he has a history of playing with, into a pit of identical balls and see which one he retrieves. In my previous property, a large section of the garden was covered in 20mm stones. My Labrador (Mr B) picked up one of the stones and dropped it on the patio. I unthinkingly threw it onto the stoned area, but Mr B went off in pursuit and returned with a stone; once again dropping it on the patio. I wondered if it might be the same stone I'd thrown, so I marked it, and once again threw the stone into the stoned area of the garden; sure enough Mr B brought back the exact same stone from an area which contained four tonnes of stones. He was almost definitely using scent (his and mine) to determine which stone was of interest. Dogs are far more brilliant than we give them credit for and can easily determine the difference between some old cushions they've repeatedly played with (and covered in saliva) and some that sit boringly on the sofa and seem to do nothing. Raising a happy puppy isn't about forcing them to behave as we want them to, regardless of their needs. It's about finding a compromise that we are all happy with.

Chewing

Chewing is a very natural thing for pups to do and it serves several functions. Firstly, chewing is a way of investigating the world and exploring tastes and textures. This is similar to the way in which humans like to touch things. Chewing is also a major part of their physical development because it is exercising and strengthening the jaw muscles and developing fine motor skills. In humans, fine motor skills are usually considered in connection with hand movements. It's the connection and development of the brain, nervous system and muscles to allow manipulation of things, like pencils or buttons. It may also be considered in relation to babies learning to eat independently or in learning to control the plethora of muscles which allow us to talk. Dogs obviously cannot hold things or manipulate them in the way humans can. If we consider this, it becomes easier to understand how important it might be for dogs to use their mouths and develop fine motor control of those jaws.

Chewing also helps the dog throughout the teething process. Puppies have 28 deciduous teeth, sometimes referred to as puppy teeth or needle teeth. Most of these will be lost between 16 to 23 weeks of age, as 42 permanent teeth begin to make an appearance. It often goes unnoticed, depending how often we look in the dog's mouth, but there is a lot going on during this period. They have periods where they don't show much interest in chewing at all, yet at other times have a very strong desire to chew. Chewing often helps to dislodge the deciduous teeth. In addition to dislodging teeth, chewing may be soothing and also provides a distraction from the discomfort of those large teeth pushing through the gums.

From the puppy's point of view, they are simply trying to fulfil behavioural urges and find relief, but very often, chewing is seen as a behaviour problem and the dog might be considered to be behaving naughtily. When I consult on behaviour cases, it's very often not a dog behaviour issue I'm dealing with. Very often it's not the dog who needs to change behaviour, but the human caregiver. It's our job, as the guardians of our dogs, to ensure their needs are met in ways which are compatible with our own needs; for example, giving the dog appropriate chew items.

However, dogs don't know the difference between what you consider to be an appropriate chew toy, and a designer handbag or iPhone. How could they? To a dog, there is no such thing as monetary value. Value comes from how interesting something is to the dog. For example, novelty, palatability, scent, and very often, the mere fact that somebody else has it, makes it quite desirable. Since Monty came to live with me, we've had regular meet-ups with one of his littermate brothers, Beor. If one of them picks up a stick, you can bet your life that the other dog will want that stick. There could be 10 sticks on the ground, but they want the one that the other dog has and will chase each other around, competing for it.

Our job then, if we don't want the legs of the dining room chairs chewed off, is to provide lots of alternatives and to keep those alternatives relevant to the dog. As a result they get to choose to chew on something which suits their needs at the time.

I use soft things, for example knotted ropes and teddy bears designed specifically for dogs; hard things like nylabones; rubbery things, like puller rings, rubber bones and Kongs; food-based chews, like Himalayan yak cheese, dried tripe, bully sticks, beef tendon, lamb's legs, and buffalo ears; wood, like Origins natural root, and olive wood. All of these items should be sourced from reputable retailers and be designed specifically for dogs. This doesn't necessarily mean they will suit your individual dog and there is always a safety aspect to consider; for example, choking, or swallowing parts that break off. For this reason, I only give these items when I'm able to supervise. You should also check the age range each particular product is suitable for.

Having a good mix of chew things to offer the dog keeps it interesting and makes it less likely they will chew your furniture, but what should we do if they are chewing up the remote control or the arm of your chair? Firstly, we should consider management. Management simply means that we set things up in a way that prevents the behaviour occurring. For example, the dog cannot chew the remote control or your iPhone if you don't leave them where she can get them. This sounds obvious; however, I've seen a number of clients who've complained that the dog had taken a liking to chewing their shoes. Why are shoes so interesting? Just think about all the scent that's inside them from your feet and all the scent on the outside from all the places they've been. Add to this the fact that they are interesting objects in their own right, with laces and tongues and different textures; then add the fact that they are just so chewable. Maybe the question we should be asking is, how could the dog not chew them? So, what is the answer to protecting those shoes? The easiest answer is to keep them out of the dog's reach, in a shoe cupboard.

It's not always possible; we can't very well move all the furniture. So what do we do if the dog chews the leg of the table? Giving the dog lots of alternatives makes this less likely to happen, but it doesn't eliminate the risk altogether. Firstly, if we are not supervising the puppy they should be in a safe space, where they can't perform unwanted behaviours. This is one of the reasons I think crates (for short periods) can be a good thing. While we're supervising the puppy, we can use alternative behaviours to replace their desire to chew something they shouldn't. If they show any interest in chewing the furniture you can distract them with something more interesting, for example a gentle game of tug, throwing a squeaky toy, giving them one of their chew items, or just having some interaction with them. In the same way that Monty and his brother desire the same stick, as soon as you start playing with a toy, the puppy is likely to want to interact too. If this doesn't work, I'd consider taking them out of the room (in a happy friendly manner) and distracting them in a different location. Dogs generally begin to ignore things which are unimportant or uninteresting to them, so over time, as long as we consistently prevent the table leg being a thing of interest (it will be interesting if the pup gets to chew it regularly) then the pup will eventually not give it a second glance.

As a real-life example of this, one of Monty's first interests in things he mustn't play with were the imitation/decorative stones on my fireplace. The fire isn't used; it's purely for decoration, but I'm not sure what the stones are made from (possible danger risk) and, in any case, I really don't want them chewed. Monty managed to pick one up on a couple of occasions. I simply gave him something better to do by squeaking soft toys and pulling them along so he would give chase. If I was close enough as he approached the stones, I'd get in the way with a more appropriate toy or chew. Within the first week, Monty stopped being interested in the stones. It was almost like he could no longer see them. However, I can almost guarantee that if I were to start moving the stones or simply pick one up and place it down again, Monty's interest would be reignited. If I need to clean things which I don't want him touching, it's wise for me to do it while he is out of the room. To some extent this phenomenon continues into adulthood, but it's far stronger in puppies; pups are very much primed to pay attention and notice what we're doing because it's part of normal developmental learning. Another option might have been to remove the stones until he's older, or even replacing the imitation stones with real stones, which are less likely to be harmful, unless you have a dog that swallows non-food items.

There are arguments which could be made against the approach of teaching pups via distraction. If the puppy gets something good for attempting to chew the table leg, doesn't this teach the pup to chew the table leg? If that were the only time you gave the good stuff or interacted in a playful way, then yes, it could reinforce the behaviour, but it's not as simple as that. The interaction with you, or other distracting, fun, behaviour, isn't contingent on the dog chewing the table leg. The dog will, over time, pay less attention to the table leg, and more attention to the other things which bring enjoyment. With this in mind, it's very important (in fact it's one of the most important points in this book) that you do not only pay attention to the dog when they are doing (or about to do) things you don't like. They should get plenty of interaction with you, and together you can build a great relationship. Sit on the floor and play with them, make their toys come alive, build positive interaction into your daily routine.

Why shouldn't we use punishment-based methods of teaching the dog not to chew? If we were to use some of the aversive methods which have been used by many people in the past; for example, shouting 'no', startling the dog (with sudden noise), spraying them in the face with water, or physically hitting the dog; apart from ethical concerns, we must consider that these things don't give the dog any information about what we want them to do. These methods simply punish perfectly natural behaviours without replacing them with an alternative. Such methods also risk causing the puppy to become anxious and/or frightened of things (including us) which they really should not feel anxious about. It goes much further than this; it could affect the dog's entire development and their relationship with us. Learning is far more difficult in an environment of fear or anxiety. Imagine you are learning to drive. Do you want a driving instructor who says 'nicely done' when we get it right? Or do you want an instructor who suddenly yells 'NO' each time you make an error? If we had the second instructor, we would soon begin to make more mistakes. Our anxiety would rise, and our confidence would fall. The thing to remember is that we get to choose our instructor, and if we don't like them we can fire them and find another. The dog doesn't get to choose; they are stuck with us - so I firmly believe it's our responsibility to do the very best we can for them.

What's in a Name?

Dogs easily learn the scent of other individuals and recognise other dogs in this way, but they don't have names for each other. It could be argued that they do have some kind of naming system going on, simply by virtue of the fact they recognise the scent of dogs they've previously met or family members and the mental recognition, memory, (or filing system, if it's easier to think of it that way) is in fact a naming system. However, it's certainly not a system which allows them to call to other individuals after deciding on a name for them.

So what does a dog's name really mean to the dog? It largely depends on how we use it, but I think most likely, from the dog's perspective, their name is simply a signal to pay attention or to come to the person who called them. Thinking of it this way, it's easy to see how their name may become confusing when it's used by the human in different ways. For example, one day the human uses the name to call the dog to give them a treat, another day they may use the name to tell the dog off. I think it's best to think about what you want their name to mean; are you calling them to you? Or do you just want them to pay attention to you, or look at you? For the best results, the dog's name should always be associated with good things. If it has been associated with bad things, or people in a bad mood, it may be more difficult for the dog when we use their name to get their attention. This is because they may begin to associate the sound of their name with both good and bad outcomes. This is what behaviourists sometimes refer to as a poisoned cue. The dog may become apprehensive in their response to the cue due to conflicting emotions. With this in mind, it is far better if we just use their name for pleasant things and never when we are cross or annoyed. However, we are only human, and it may happen from time to time; for example, if the dog knocks over your expensive lamp you are probably going to be slightly annoyed and use their name to chastise them. We are human, it happens, we sometimes find it difficult to control our emotions.

From the dog's perspective, however, they probably got a scare from the crashing lamp, and a second scare from our overt displeasure. This doesn't help them, and it doesn't help us; when something goes wrong in the future, perhaps something startles the dog, we don't want them thinking that we are going to get angry. We really want them to trust and feel completely safe with us. We want to be their safe haven. The best approach I've found is to see the funny side when things go wrong, then later, when things have calmed down, we can re-evaluate and consider what we might do differently in the future to ensure lamps (or whatever) cannot so easily be knocked over.

Many dogs will naturally learn their name. They will learn that when you say 'Monty' (or whatever the dog is called), it's a good idea to pay attention because something good is about to unfold. You could simply say 'Monty' when you are about to interact with them, pick up a toy and play a game, or drop a few treats on the floor. As long as the dog enjoys these things, they should quickly learn the association and pay attention when you call.

So, what if it's not working? What if they are ignoring your calls? Firstly, it's important to try to see things from the dog's perspective. What reasons could there be for them to be uninterested or unresponsive to their name? As discussed, we should ensure the name is not being used to scold the dog in any way. Secondly, are the things you're doing truly enjoyable and reinforcing for the dog? Even if they are reinforcing (enjoyable) to begin with, this may not always be the case. For example, imagine you say the dog's name, then give a piece of food. The dog may be very keen to begin with, but at some point, if we continually repeated this, the dog would reach satiation point, meaning they've had enough – so continuing might not be so rewarding to them and could even become more of a nuisance. With this in mind, it's wise to keep monitoring the interest levels and stop well before they lose their enthusiasm (which might depend on what the particular food is). Thirdly, are people repeatedly saying the dog's name when they are busy elsewhere.

For example, Monty comes to the office with me a few days per week - he would go around the desks saying hello to everyone, and they were all pleased to see him, so he got a lot of fuss. One of the office workers would constantly call his name when he was happily getting a fuss elsewhere. On the first few occasions he responded and went to find the person who was calling him, at which point she would simply say 'Hello,

Monty'. She just seemed to take pleasure from the fact that he came to look for her when she called. However, from Monty's perspective, he had just left the person who was giving him a fuss to find that the lady calling him didn't actually have anything of interest; she just liked calling him. He soon stopped responding when she called, because it was meaningless, or at least, it wasn't worth leaving what he was doing for. But dogs are very smart beings indeed. Monty did not stop responding to his name in any other situation; he just learnt to ignore Betty, much to her disappointment. What we might consider is this: if we wanted to teach a dog to ignore a particular person calling them, we might ensure that it wasn't rewarding to pay attention to the call, while also ensuring that doing an alternative behaviour (greeting other people) was rewarding. In other words, Monty had been inadvertently trained to ignore the call and attended to other things.

Think about what lessons can be taken from this. Whenever you are trying to get your dog's attention, especially in the early stages of learning, it is best to wait until they are not engrossed in another activity. For example, at five months of age, Monty has a very good recall; I can blow my whistle or call his name and he will come running. However, there are times, like when he is in full-on play mode with another dog, when the recall might fail. It's important not to keep repeating a failing recall because we are then teaching the dog that it is insignificant. Wait for an opportune moment, when there is a break in play, to get their attention; give them a nice treat and let them go back to playing. Over time, this is what will build a better, more reliable, recall. This is explained in greater depth in the recall chapter.

Socialisation and Habituation

Socialisation and habituation are often misunderstood. Socialisation refers to the pup's ability to form social bonds and relationships with those around them. The term has also been used as an umbrella term for getting the puppy used to their environment and all things in it. Others argue that this is not socialisation, because the puppy isn't socialising with all of these things, for example, the noise of traffic. Therefore, the term *habituation* is used to describe these (non-social) experiences. Technically, this term is also not entirely accurate because *habituation* means to steadily reduce a startle response. For example, if you hear a gunshot nearby, you may flinch – if you hear the gunshot every minute, the startle response will reduce, because you get used to it and stop recognising it as a threat. This isn't what we do with puppies. With puppies we are trying to introduce them to the world at a rate that will not cause a startle response in the first place.

It doesn't matter that the terms aren't technically accurate. We can still accept that what is generally meant by the terms socialisation and habituation is that we are getting the puppy ready for the life ahead of them – we're ensuring (or trying to ensure) they are well adjusted, sociable, beings, able to live in a human world without being overly fearful or anxious.

But what does this mean in reality? Ideally, it means they are unafraid of other dogs to the degree that they can enjoy their company, or at least be unconcerned by their presence. It means they are not overly concerned by your neighbour's cat, or the sound of a dustcart, or fireworks. It's about acclimatising them to their environment. You may have noticed the obvious problem – we do not live in an ideal world. It's not possible to introduce them to everything they might encounter, and some will be more anxious than others purely through their genetics or an early traumatic event. There is not a one-size-fits-all formula for socialisation or habituation. Some people have even taken the idea of socialisation to extremes and suggest things like meeting 100 men in hats, and seeing 100 pushchairs, etc. before 12 weeks of age. Actually, taking the idea of socialisation to extremes may cause more stress and anxiety rather than prevent it.

One of the things I often see mentioned for socialisation and habituation training is taking the puppy to a cafe. In some situations that might make sense – it was one of the required tasks when I was an assistance dog trainer. Assistance dogs often need to be accustomed to that sort of environment, but for many of us, when are we planning on taking our dog to a cafe? I'm not! I never use cafes. For me, it was important that Monty wasn't concerned by elevators, because my office is on the 3rd floor. For other people they may never need to take their dog anywhere near an elevator. It is, therefore, a very individual plan for each of us. We don't always know what life has in store just around the corner, so it may sometimes be prudent to prepare for other environments, but we should be careful not to overwhelm the puppy. Think about the things which are most important and concentrate on those first.

These days puppy breeders are often very good at beginning the puppy's socialisation and habituation. This can make a tremendous difference to the pup's entire life. Monty came to me from such a breeder. He was already very accustomed to the outside world; he was sociable and confident. The breeder had both of Monty's parents living on the property and I think it's very helpful if the pup has interacted with another adult dog, rather than just the littermates and mum, which is a very unique relationship. Our job is to continue the development which has already begun.

One of the biggest mistakes I see is that people, keen to introduce the pup to everything, almost force the environment on to them. Force is never a good thing because it removes choice. If you have choices, you will have less anxiety. For example, imagine you can't swim but you're forced to jump into water without knowing how deep it is. To jump or be pushed are your only options – how does that feel? I imagine for a non-swimmer it's a terrifying prospect. Now imagine it's your choice to go into the water or not. You may choose not to do it; after all, you can't swim, but the difference is, you are not afraid. You're not afraid because you have a choice. Over time, having a choice will build your confidence. You may get close and look into the water; you may dip a toe in; you might realise it's shallow and go for a paddle. The confidence to do so comes from having a choice – you know you're not about to be pushed straight in. You are no longer afraid for your life. It may well have been quicker if your friend had pushed you in – you might have learned the water was shallow this way, but you will be more hesitant of going anywhere near water with that friend in the future and you didn't learn how to safely evaluate the risk.

This happens with dogs all the time – we very often fail to give them time to evaluate and make choices. I've lost count of the number of times I see dogs being dragged away from something; maybe they are standing still looking at a deer or a rabbit or a man in an unusual hat, and then suddenly they're pulled in the opposite direction. If it is safe to do so, I always allow the dog to stop and look. It's a very natural behaviour and they are likely evaluating how interesting or how dangerous something is, but if we pull them away, they lose the opportunity to learn, or to feel okay about the distant object. They lose the ability to make good choices and they lose the opportunity to disengage by themselves.

Introductions

Give your puppy choices; obviously you must ensure their safety, but let them learn about their environment at their own pace. Allow them to be unsure about things – we have no need to force them to say hi to strangers or shopping carts or anything else. If they are allowed to be unsure, perhaps taking a few steps towards the object or person and moving back again, this may give them the confidence to approach, but if you give them no choices – if they know there is no moving away – they are essentially trapped, become more fearful of new situations, and lack trust in you to be their safe haven. It's important to introduce them to the things they will encounter, but it really isn't a numbers game. Quality of the experience is far more important than quantity.

Socialisation with dogs

This may look very different, depending on where you live. Many places have strict leash laws prohibiting off-leash dogs. Leashes (although they often give the human a sense of safety) may prevent natural interaction and can cause issues; for example, the phenomena of on-leash reactivity. It's easy to see how they can prevent natural behaviours; for example, the dogs' ability to circle around each other. I've seen tangled leads many times, and for this reason it is reasonably common in my location that training classes prohibit on-leash greeting. We all must do the best we can, but my view is that dogs will learn the social skills far easier if they get off-leash opportunities to interact with other dogs. We do need to be picky though and ensure they meet sensible, confident, adult dogs with good social skills as well as a few puppies for play in safe areas. I have been very fortunate in this regard, Monty is excellent at reading other dogs and if they don't want to play, he knows it and moves on. I have never before had a young dog with this level of dog socialisation skills. I believe this is, at least partly, due to having more than one adult dog in his life whilst with his breeder. Too often, but understandably, we want to wrap the puppy in a protective cocoon. This might prevent us giving them the opportunities to interact and learn dog social skills, and in the long term, cause anxiety, because they don't feel able to interact with other dogs peacefully. However, things are never so simple. There are many stories of dogs becoming dog reactive following a bad experience; we must be ever vigilant and do what we can to ensure we avoid coming into contact with seriously aggressive dogs. I wish it were otherwise, but this is something all responsible dog guardians fear.

How can we possibly do this? One option is to choose walking areas that make it easier and avoid places where known aggressive dogs are walked. I drive to an area out of town where I've never met any seriously aggressive dogs. It's also quite open so I can see people (and dogs) at a distance and decide if I want to get closer. I also tend to go for the main walk of the day quite early, so there are fewer people around. I realise this is a luxury many will not have, but it is just about trying to minimise risk in whatever way we can.

You may be able to arrange meet-ups with dog friends you are comfortable with and book private, enclosed, fields together. Although our aim is to socialise the puppy to the world around them, it's also our responsibility to try and keep them out of harm's way. I don't worry too much about looking odd or rude, if I'm not comfortable with the dogs or people coming towards me, I turn and walk away.

Anthropomorphism & Emotions

Anthropomorphism is a word everybody who's ever mentioned their dog's feelings has heard. It's the attribution of human characteristics to animals, or any other non-human entity. Traditionally, it's been assumed that it's wrong to anthropomorphise. Humans tend to see animals as very separate from themselves.

If the animal does not possess the characteristic being attributed to them, it can lead to problems in our relationship with them, and in how we treat them. For example, clients have sometimes told me their dog urinates in the house, out of spite, because they'd been left home alone. I don't believe the dog's emotional repertoire extends to spite; that seems to be a uniquely human characteristic. However, as I stated in the introduction to this book, they absolutely do share our primary emotions of SEEKING (enthusiasm and anticipation), RAGE (anger), FEAR (anxiety), LUST (sexual arousal), CARE (nurture), GRIEF, (sadness), and PLAY (joy). Therefore, it is not necessarily wrong to attribute human-like characteristics to animals. They may not have all the characteristics of humans, but that doesn't mean they have none.

It is often seen as an error to anthropomorphise – but this idea may cause more harm than good. To empathise with the dog, to understand the dog, to be fair to the dog, and to respect the dog as a much-loved member of the family, we absolutely must consider their emotions. Traditionally, we've failed dogs in this regard. We very often attempt to change the dog's behaviour operantly. This is the idea that if the dog gets a reinforcer (something he likes) for sitting on the rug, he will be more likely to sit on the rug in future. If he receives a punisher (something he doesn't like) for sitting on the rug, he will be less likely to sit there in future.

It sounds logical, and it is logical. But there's a problem! The dog isn't a computer where a particular input will always result in a particular output. Computers, famously, do not have emotions – dogs do! There is no doubt that operant conditioning works, but it's very much dependent on the dog's underlying emotional state. Behaviour depends on emotions. Imagine it's 2:30 AM and you hear a noise – it sounds like there's an intruder in your house; your senses are heightened; you hear the staircase creak; is this a good time to learn how to knit? Or maybe finish that crossword puzzle you've been working on? Of course not! All you will be able to focus on is the fear. This is absolutely the same for dogs. They are probably not afraid of the stairs creaking at 2:30 AM, but imagine the immense fear some dogs have during firework season. I've seen dogs that tremble, drool, and pant for hour after hour during fireworks. It's easy to see this wouldn't be a good time to teach the dog, or even to get them to perform particular behaviour they already know. For example, they may love to play fetch, but they are not likely to love it while experiencing such a high degree of fear/panic.

Lower levels of anxiety often go unnoticed by dog guardians and some dog trainers. We often just expect them to 'obey' our wishes without considering their needs or emotional state. Dog training classes are a good example of this. It is quite common for people to find their dog will do behaviours at home but refuse to do them in the training class. The most likely cause is anxiety or over-arousal. Many years back, before I was a dog trainer/behaviourist, I remember a nine-month-old German Shepherd named Samson. Samson could easily perform a down-stay while his guardian walked the length of a football field, before calling him. In the training hall, Brian (Samson's guardian) couldn't get more than five paces without Samson breaking the down-stay.

Everyone found it amusing, but what was never addressed was the anxiety Samson was obviously feeling about being in an enclosed, echoey, space with twenty other dogs. Not only were Samson's emotional needs ignored, but they were made worse; Brian was instructed to yell at him each time he broke the down-stay. Now you have an anxious dog who isn't permitted to do the one thing he needs to do in order to cope – Samson was punished for seeking safety with his human. I'd begun to learn a little about behaviour – I'd read *The Culture Clash* by Jean Donaldson, a book that would change my life, but I wasn't yet confident enough to interfere. After trying every training class in my area, I finally gave up and began my own journey into animal behaviour. There are now some excellent group classes around, but there are also some pretty awful ones who base our relationship with dogs on being able to intimidate them – that's not a relationship I'm interested in.

Samson's behaviour was the result of his emotional state. Any attempt to teach him obedience tasks, without addressing these underlying issues was doomed to fail and/or cause greater anxiety, resulting in additional problems. For example, I once consulted on a case where it was reported that the dog was aggressive when the guardian tried to put their harness on. Tracing this problem back and looking at the dog's history, the behaviour had probably begun by the dog being forced to walk past a particular spot where she'd encountered an aggressive dog six months previously. Following this event, she wanted to turn left on leaving the house, but the guardian had insisted they walk to the right.

From the dog's point of view, she is avoiding danger and looking for coping strategies, but a lack of appreciation for her emotional state led to her avoiding going through the door, then avoidance of the leash, then avoidance of the harness, then ignoring the guardian, and finally, snapping at the guardian – she had become untrusting because they hid the harness behind their back. During a stress response, adrenaline (epinephrine) and noradrenaline (norepinephrine) are released causing increased heart rate, blood pressure and muscle force – the digestive system shuts down to save energy, there's a heightened alertness and pain receptors are dulled. This isn't the time to be training – from the dog's perspective, it's about staying alive.

When we fail to recognise the dog's emotional state, we make life more difficult for them and for ourselves. We receive an awful lot of emotional support from the dog – we just need to give some back.

The Vacuum Cleaner and other Exciting Things

I've lost count of the number of times people have told me their dog is reactive toward the vacuum cleaner. This can take different forms, from wanting to play with it, to a defensive/aggressive kind of reactivity. The same thing sometimes occurs with other household objects, for example brooms. The vacuum cleaner is noisy, which may cause the puppy to be unsure about it. If the breeder has done a good job, your puppy may not be bothered by such noises, but the back-and-forth movement we make as we use the vacuum is likely to be irresistible to a young puppy. The instinct to chase movement can be very strong and is present, to some degree, in all breeds.

When the pup shows interest in the movement of the vacuum cleaner, the human often finds it amusing and begins chasing the pup with the vacuum, or just pushes it quickly towards them. It may be tempting when the pup is 12 weeks of age to let them play with the vacuum cleaner, but by the time a large breed reaches 6 months of age, you probably will not want them trying to bite the vacuum cleaner while you're trying to clean the house. The stimulation of this game can easily become too much, and many small breeds may find it quite threatening to have this huge, noisy, contraption coming toward them. It is far better, never to begin this game in the first place. Don't be tempted to chase the dog with the vacuum cleaner. What most of us really want, is for the dog to find it boring and pay no attention. The first time I vacuumed with Monty in the house, sure enough, he thought it would be a great thing to chase it around. If I'd tried to use punishment, perhaps yelling or tapping him on the nose (please don't ever do that), what might I achieve? I might, if it worked, stop him playing with the vacuum cleaner. But why? How would that happen? What's the mechanism? What association would he have made that keeps him away? The most probable association would be that, when the vacuum cleaner is present, I'm aggressive towards him. I want the best relationship I can have with him; I certainly don't want him developing a fear of the vacuum cleaner or of me. These fears sometimes begin in such innocuous ways but then develop into major problems. I didn't get a puppy to make him frightened or cautious of me. We can do so much better than this.

When I vacuum, I give Monty something better to do. I give him a long-lasting chew treat. He was perfectly happy to have his chew and chose not to chase the vacuum cleaner and, over a short period of time, has learnt to ignore it completely. It will not always be so easy. Some pups may prefer to chase the vacuum cleaner than chew the treat. Our job is to make the right choice easier for them. Perhaps give the treat in one room and vacuum in an adjoining room with a child gate on the doorway. The objective is firstly to ensure we are not encouraging the problem to develop (by chasing them with the vacuum cleaner) and secondly to make it easy for them to choose to do something else.

Destroying Their Toys

As an advocate of canine enrichment 'my dog destroys her toys' is something I hear a lot. I can certainly understand the frustration. Many of the enrichment toys are expensive, and to have them not even last the day is disappointing, to say the least.

In the shops, I often see notices displayed beside the toys, stating something like 'THESE TOYS ARE NOT INDESTRUCTIBLE.' They obviously have a fair few disappointed customers. So the first thing to note is that if your dog destroys his toys, you are not alone. The reason you are not alone is that chewing is an innate behaviour of dogs; it's a genetic predisposition. Your dog isn't faulty, naughty, or bad; he's good at chewing; he's good at being a dog.

You can stop there if you'd like and just not buy things he is capable of chewing to destruction. Maybe try some of the toughest toys like Nylabone, Kong Extreme, GoughNuts or West Paw; these are tough, but nothing is truly indestructible. However, there's also plenty you can do to reduce the likelihood of toys being chewed to destruction.

Don't just give the toy to the puppy and walk away. Watch how he interacts with it. If he thinks the fun is in chewing it up, then that's what he's going to do. Maybe stick around and make the toy fun in other ways, like chasing it around, playing fetch or tug.

If you have difficulty getting the toy back from the dog, have two similar toys. Play with your dog using one toy; when you want him to leave it make the other toy the interesting one by playing with that one and paying no attention to the dog's toy. They often want what somebody else has and will leave their toy to play with the interesting one (it's your job to make it the interesting one). The toy, therefore, is not being destroyed and you can keep swapping in this way without ever having to take the toy away.

Often, it's enrichment feeding toys that people report their dogs are destroying. Strictly speaking, they are not really toys because the dog isn't playing but he's getting something interesting to do (enrichment) as he works out how to access the food. We will stick with the term 'toy' for ease. We need to ensure that the dog is introduced to this type of feeding in an appropriate way. A way which gets him focusing on the food rather than destroying the toy. The idea is that we start off as easy as possible for the dog to be successful; you can always build up the challenge later on.

Let's take two examples of how this might work.

Example 1: Using a Kong

Start off by filling it with loose food. This will fall out very easily allowing him to be successful and learn that the idea is to get the food. Over time the challenge can be increased by adding wet food, then compacted wet food and then, when the puppy's older, wet food, compacted and frozen, but I wouldn't do this until about six months of age. If at stage one the dog didn't show any interest, we could make things even easier by smearing a favourite food on the outside of the Kong. Once the food has gone you should remove the toy. Leaving it out risks the dog chewing it. I don't like the idea of dogs thinking I'm taking their things (it can induce resource guarding) so I save some of their food and sprinkle it on the floor. While they are occupied with the extra game of finding all the sprinkles, I remove the Kong trouble-free.

Example 2: Using a snuffle mat

It's been reported to me that some dogs ignore the mat or they pick it up and all the bits of food fall out. For either problem, you can make it easier by placing the mat down but just putting food on the edge, a few inches from the mat. Over a period of time, you can move the food closer to the mat. Then onto the edges of the mat, then all over the mat, then just under the top pieces of fleece and finally right into the depths of the mat.

As with the Kong, you should remove the mat when it's not being used. Throughout the process, the dog is learning that the toy represents food. The food is very easy to acquire so that becomes the focus. The toy is really only a cue to the dog that food is available.

If the dog shows little interest interacting with enrichment feeding toys it is most likely to be that the task is simply too difficult because it's not been introduced slowly enough, or the dog simply thinks that the reward isn't worth the effort.

Training – sort of!

When I was planning this book, the idea was to emphasise the number of things that do not fall under the usual consideration of training, but are vitally important. I wasn't so interested in explaining how to train sit, stay, lie down, etc. I was more interested in explaining how to raise a happy and content dog. People have often been obsessed with teaching the traditional tasks and focusing solely on obedience. However, I believe we are at the dawning of a new era. An era where the dog's welfare comes before their ability to perform obedience tasks.

Obedience training, done right, can be great fun and relationship building, but it is not the most important thing to the dog; the most important thing to a dog (other than biological needs) is feeling safe in their environment. Some training (actually, it's more accurate to call it conditioning) can help the dog lead a happier life; for example, socialisation, habituation, and conditioning to reduce the likelihood of separation anxiety.

I believe it remains important to do some training, even if we are not keen on obedience style training, which might help out the dog and the human. This book is very much about seeing things from a dog-centric position, but we also have to live in the real world. Deciding what we should train must also suit the human. We are responsible for the dog and if we don't feel able to safely manage their behaviour, we are on a very slippery slope where neither the dog or human is likely to feel happy or content.

It is too easy to get into training behaviours that are not necessarily helpful to you or the dog. We often train things just because it's what has always been done, and maybe that's fine if you're both enjoying it, but what really matters to you? What do you need from the dog? Do you really need them to sit before getting a treat? That's just an example, actually the majority of dogs seem to learn this by themselves. I remember being in a training class many years ago – we all left our dogs, in a down-stay, in the training area for 10 minutes while we waited out of sight. Today, I regret doing that exercise. My dog could do it, but what did he make of it? What did he make of me vanishing and not being permitted to follow? What did he make of being left with 12 dogs he wasn't permitted to interact with? I can't think of anything more unnatural than 12 dogs all waiting, surrounded by other waiting dogs, all a little (or a lot) anxious. What was it for? When would I ever need him to do that? Never! I never needed him to do that, other than there in that training class and I'm pretty sure he wasn't having a good time. It was a pointless exercise that just caused a little anxiety.

I no longer train pointless exercises. I do train exercises that seem to have no point, but they are for fun, for interacting with each other, for building a good relationship – they are never to show off how long my dog can tolerate something he doesn't enjoy. There are many ways to train a dog to do a particular behaviour, but the question is, how do you want them to feel about doing the behaviour? Good training isn't just about getting the dog to do something – it's about getting them to enjoy doing it.

Make a list of the behaviours which are important to you, and maybe think about why they're important. The priorities for me are:

Leave it
Wait
Not jumping up
Recall
Walking

These will be discussed in the following chapters, along with why they're my priorities.

Leave it/Drop it

'Leave it' is an exercise which will teach your pup to drop an item when asked. It's an important exercise because we may need the dog to drop dangerous items, or things they shouldn't have. If we simply grab items from the dog, we may inadvertently encourage them to run away with forbidden objects or resource guard them. In some cases, the anxiety of having things snatched from them may even encourage them to swallow inedible items.

It's very useful to be able to easily get the dog to drop items that they shouldn't have or just to give you back a ball or let go of a tug toy. However, we should be clear what the 'leave it' means. People will often use it to mean 'drop it' – 'don't pick that up' – 'stop looking at that cat' – 'don't sniff that dog'. If we teach our dog that 'leave it' means let go of what is in your mouth, it's a little confusing if the next day we expect 'leave it' to mean 'stop paying attention to that dog'. From the dog's perspective, you're telling them to drop something they don't have – and then we wonder why they struggle! If we are not consistent with what 'leave it' means, how can we expect our dogs to know what it means? Actually, if we were to use the words 'drop it' it may prevent us from inadvertently using the term for other purposes and causing confusion or watering down the word's meaning.

The 'leave it' cue is also often said harshly, like we are reprimanding the dog. 'Leave it' should not be a battle of wills between us and the dog. It is a cue for the dog to let go of something in order to gain reinforcement. If the dog is not letting go then the reason is not that we need to apply more force, it's a sign that we need to apply more training at an easier (for the dog to succeed) level. In the following protocol we will stick with the cue 'drop it' but you may use whatever you prefer, as long as it's consistent and not said harshly.

1.　With the dog close by, drop approximately five treats on the floor. If they are keen to eat them, we can move on to the next step. If they're not keen, you might need to up your game and get some better treats.

2.　Say 'drop it' and drop your treats on the floor. Repeat five times per day for three days. We can add a verbal cue early in this exercise because we know from step 1 that we are highly likely to get the behaviour that we want. At this stage all we are asking is for the dog to come and eat the treats. She doesn't actually have hold of anything. We are teaching her that, for now, 'drop it' means treats are available.

3.　Repeat step 2 but this time say 'drop it' only when the dog has something in their mouth which they will need to let go of in order to eat the treats. We must ensure that we don't make this too difficult so start by having the dog drop items which are not of high value (to the dog) to begin with and move on to higher valued items slowly over several days or weeks.

Note: We should resist the temptation to grab hold of the dropped item the moment it's released. Be casual;

act like the dropped item is of no interest to you. The dog can go back to it after having the treats. In the dog's mind this may give greater value to dropping an item to get the treats. This is because they didn't lose the original item – they got both. This method is for developing a strong inclination to drop. There will be a time when we must retrieve the dropped item, maybe because it's a dangerous item the dog should not have. In these situations, we can drop a second lot of treats or maybe distract the dog in other ways, perhaps with a favourite toy or luring the dog to another area. Maybe you have nothing at hand to give to the dog, but if you have practiced well the dog will be very accustomed to dropping their item and paying attention to you, it's always worked out well for them in the past.

The Swap It - Drop It

This is another method of teaching a dog to drop items out of their mouth. Ideally for this method, you will use two identical tug toys, but it is not absolutely essential.

1. Keep one toy hidden behind your back and get the puppy interested in the other tug toy by wiggling it around on the floor. This is best done kneeling down and should only be done with a dog you know very well and is very comfortable with such proximity. Really make the toy come alive so that the pup chases it and eventually catches it.

2. Have a gentle game of tug for 5 - 10 seconds and then stop tugging. Instantly bring the hidden toy from

behind your back and bring this one to life by wiggling it around the floor. Dogs will almost always want the toy you bring to life. They let go of the first toy to give chase to the second toy. You can swap back and forth between the toys in this way and each time, they will come and play with the interesting one.

3. Repeat step 2 but this time introduce the cue word ('drop it') as you stop playing with the active toy and fractionally before introducing the other, bringing it to life and encouraging play.

4. Repeat step 3 but delay the time between saying 'drop it' and beginning to play with the second toy. We may increase this from one second to five or six seconds over several days. This should create a level of control and focus rather than the dog jumping straight from one toy to the other.

Wait (your emergency stop)

Emergency Stop training gives us the ability to quickly stop the dog and get them to stand waiting for a further instruction. In reality, it will mainly be used for fun, but could one day save the dog's life. If the day comes when your dog is running towards a dangerous situation, it will at least give you a chance of stopping them. There are no guarantees. A spooked, frightened, or otherwise excited animal may behave in unexpected ways. Safety should be our priority. No amount of training practice can match or replace the need for us to keep our dogs safe and reduce risk through management. However, sometimes dangerous situations arise which could not have been foreseen. Being able to stop the dog in such situations is very handy.

This exercise is one where I add a verbal cue right from the start. More often I train in silence and add words later, if needed. The cue I use is 'wait.' Many trainers use the word 'stop' but I think 'stop' is a harsher word and we can more easily find ourselves yelling at the dog as though we were telling them off, rather than giving them a cue to stand still for a moment. To begin with, the word 'wait' is meaningless to the dog. We will first teach them it indicates special treats are available. It begins a little like the leave it/drop it exercise. The way in which we deliver the treats is the thing that will teach the dog to stop and watch us.

1.   With the dog reasonably close and paying attention to you, say 'wait' and immediately drop a nice treat on the ground for the dog. Repeat five times. Break off for a while, then repeat the entire process again. The dog should soon learn that whenever you say 'wait' a tasty treat is coming.

2.   You may now practise the procedure when the dog is close by but not paying direct attention to you. Perhaps they are sniffing or looking the other way. Say 'wait' and instantly chuck the treat to the dog. This is so they don't learn to run straight back to you to get it. Let them go back to sniffing (or whatever) and repeat. Try to do about five repetitions at least three times per day for three days.

3.   Repeat step 2 but this time do not throw the treat until the dog's attention has turned to you. They should look towards you waiting for the treat to come towards them. The second they look towards you, throw the treat. We want to throw the treat before the dog feels inclined to move towards us. It's important that the reinforcer comes for just looking towards us rather than moving towards us. If we reinforce moving towards us, then that's what we will teach, rather than teaching them to remain stationary.

4.   Increase the time that the dog waits (focused on you) before throwing the food. Maybe start at 1 second and increase by 1 second each time you train, up to around 20 seconds. At this point it's prudent to vary the duration, for example, a 5 second wait, followed by a 3 second wait, followed by a 15 then a 7 second wait.

This will help prevent the dog from predicting you and will help to keep their focus. If they always waited 20 seconds, there may be no need to concentrate on you because nothing ever happened in that 20 second gap. You can continue, further increasing the duration if you wish, but I like to keep it fun and interesting for the dog, so I rarely take this exercise beyond 20 seconds.

Note: If you consistently throw the food short, the dog may predict this and move forward before you intended. A similar thing happens if you consistently throw past the dog's position. Unless you are a crack shot and consistently reach the dog with the treat, it may be best to mix it up, throwing long, short, left and right so that the dog never knows where it's going next.

It may also be wise to walk to the dog and treat by hand occasionally. This may be needed in a genuine emergency so it's a good idea to practise it. You can extend this to clipping the leash back on and treating. You may also add a release word, for example 'go on then' just before tossing the treat. Practise the emergency stop in different environments to proof it and get a strong behaviour. When changing environments, we need to begin training at an easier level and build it up again. You may make further use of this exercise at home by asking your dog to wait as you open a door or any time you need them to stand still for a moment.

Remember you are training a puppy, they are just a baby with a fast developing brain – keep it fun. I generally train the 'wait' from about 4 months of age.

Not Jumping up at People

A reasonably common problem for people with friendly dogs is that the dog is overenthusiastic in their greeting of people. The dog's entire focus is on jumping all over us when we get home. It's also reasonably common for them to jump up at visitors. From the dog's perspective, it's all very exciting, and guess what? people love it; or at least they love it when it's a little puppy jumping up – they love the fact that this tiny baby is so excited to see them. But then what? What happens when the tiny Labrador turns into a 35 kilo adult. Then they don't like it so much! The dog is just doing what they were encouraged to do. The thing to remember is that, if you don't want your adult dog to jump all over you, don't encourage them to do so as a puppy. We will not actually be teaching the puppy not to jump up. Not doing something, isn't a behaviour so how could we ever teach it? We'll be focusing on the behaviour we want instead – that's something you can teach.

When I'm sitting in a chair, Monty will often place his front feet up on me. I don't mind this at all. In fact, I quite like it – I give him a stroke and talk to him. I don't want him to jump up at me when I'm standing up or when I walk through the door. Traditional advice was to ignore the dog when they jump up or if they are excited to see you. I think this is damaging to the relationship and unfair on the puppy. Greetings are important to dogs, and most other canids. It is part of the bonding process and feeling safe as a family unit.

It is fine to make a fuss of them when you arrive home, but if you don't want them to jump up, how about you kneel down? Perhaps have a tug toy handy to play a little game. You never need to punish them for jumping up, you only need to ensure that better things happen when their feet are on the floor.

Sometimes it's our guests the dog jumps all over. Once again, the traditional advice has often been to ask the guest to ignore the dog until they calm down. If you've ever tried this, you may have discovered the problem with it; humans find it incredibly difficult to ignore a cute dog who's lavishing adoration on them. The best and easiest solution I've found is simply to give the dog an enrichment toy stuffed with their food or a snuffle mat. They may still be a little excited, but the ritual of jumping all over guests will change. The guest will become the predictor that the dog gets to have their enrichment toys. The pup is choosing a different behaviour.

If you have a very friendly dog who thinks it's their job to say hi to everyone outside of the home, remember that sometimes people don't like dogs, or they are afraid of them, or they just don't want a wet nose shoved into their hand. In this case, whenever you see a person approaching, start giving the dog treats, one after another until the person has passed. The dog will soon learn that people approaching mean treats from you will rain down. When they've learned this and their focus is on you, you may reduce the number of treats so they wait two seconds, then three, then four. Before long you may only need one treat. If they are looking at you for the treat, they are not throwing themselves at other people. It's not about trying to give treats whilst the dog is reacting to the other person in full 'I'm going to jump on you' mode. We are waiting until the dog's focus is with us, we are reinforcing the choice that the dog made and we are reinforcing the preferred behaviour. It will work better if you start at a distance where the dog doesn't try to say hi, and reduce the distance over time; give people a wide berth at the start of training.

Recall

We have already discussed an informal, more natural, way of conditioning the recall in the section on teaching the puppy their name. That may be all you ever need, however, dogs failing to recall to their guardian when called is one of the biggest concerns for dog lovers and is also a safety concern. With this in mind, the following instructions are a more structured approach which many will find useful, even if your dog has already begun to ignore you when you call.

There are great benefits to having a very good recall. The dog gets to have more off-leash (where permitted) time and interact with the environment more naturally. However, we should always consider that no recall can be considered to be 100% reliable. We have no way of knowing how a sudden, unusual, or unexpected occurrence might affect the dog. For example, I was walking in a local woodland recently with Monty when a motocross motorcycle came hurtling towards us.

Monty was about 100 feet away from me. He was well used to loud noises and traffic, but in the woodland, it was totally unexpected. By the time I called him to me, he was already having a bit of a panic and ran the other way, totally ignoring his, usually, very good recall. This was my error. I should have put in the recall much earlier when I heard the motorcycle in the distance, but like Monty, I wasn't expecting them to ride through the woodland. Monty was still very young, but actually, I think it could happen at any age. Even if he was much more experienced; it is still possible that sudden panic would cause him to run in the wrong direction. There is no such thing as a 100% recall. It comes down to circumstances. We can produce an excellent recall, but I do not think we should ever believe that it cannot fail. We need to consider the implications and evaluate risk factors. I often see people walking dogs off-leash by the roadside. Even with all my experience in the world of training animals, I would absolutely never take this risk, and Monty only goes off-leash well away from roads.

Even in places of safety, and without unusual events or distractions, I very often see people struggling to get their dog to come back to them. One of the biggest problems is that when these people finally get the dog back, they are angry, so it's not a pleasant experience for the dog. From the dog's perspective, they are returning to an angry human who puts them on-leash, chastises them, and stomps away. That's not really something the dog can look forward to returning for, so it makes a good recall harder and harder to achieve. I completely understand that it's frustrating, but we really need to show our dogs that we are a safe haven if we expect them to trust us.

My general procedure for ensuring dogs learn that returning is an excellent thing to do is as follows. For ease of writing, let's assume the dog's name is Fido.

Fido may have already learned to ignore the sound of your voice when you recall him outdoors. If this is the case, I suggest using a whistle; I use a gun-dog whistle

(Acme Dog 211.5) because it's a nice sound and a good tone for dogs. Where the following instructions call for a treat to be given, use a small piece of chicken, or other meaty treat that Fido really enjoys. Food treats should be approximately the size of a fingernail to allow for lots of training without the dog overeating or getting bored with the food. Food treats could also be replaced by a favourite toy for some dogs (common with Border Collies and other hard-working breeds). In fact, some dogs so enjoy the exhilaration of being released to go and play, that this becomes reinforcement for coming back when called; treats will likely make the training process much easier.

When should you move from one step to another?
If Fido is responding well at least 4 out of 5 times you may proceed to the next step.

If Fido is responding well 3 out of 5 times, repeat the step.

If Fido is responding well less than 3 out of 5 times, go back to the previous step.

I'll assume that you are using a whistle, but you don't have to; you could also use any distinctive word or sound, if it's different from any cue the dog has already learned to ignore.

Step 1: With Fido nearby (indoors), blow the whistle and give a treat. Repeat 15 times per day for three days. I've tried many different whistle patterns over the years. I find a very short pip, immediately followed by a longer pip, works best. So each time you blow you are doing two pips, one short and one long.

Step 2: Within the home and with Fido further away from you, perhaps the other side of the room, blow the whistle and give a treat as soon as Fido reaches you. Repeat 10 times per day for three days.

Step 3: Within the home and with Fido in another room from you, blow the whistle and give a treat as soon as Fido reaches you. Repeat 10 times per day for three days.

Step 4: Within the garden, blow the whistle and give a treat as soon as Fido reaches you. Repeat 10 times per day for three days.

Step 5: In a safe area outside of the home, and with Fido still on the leash, blow the whistle and give a treat. Repeat five times.

Step 6: Within the safe area, remove the leash and allow Fido to have a run around for five minutes before you begin training. Continue with Fido running free (as long as it is safe to do so) but each time he comes within five paces blow the whistle and give a treat. Immediately allow Fido to continue running free. Repeat 10 to 15 times for three days. This step may be completed with a long line attached to his harness if you do not have a very safe area. You must also consider local leash laws.

Step 7: Over the next 10 (approximately) training sessions repeat the instructions for step six but gradually increase Fido's distance from you when you blow the whistle. So you may increase the distance by five paces per training session.

Step 8: Repeat steps six and seven with added distractions (this will be easier to do with the help of a friend and their dog). Maybe a dog on the other side of the field which is too far away to distract him too much.

Step 9: Repeat steps six and seven but increase the distractions slightly. Perhaps a little nearer to the distraction.

Step 10: Continue to add distractions in small increments. Perhaps getting closer to them or even playing with another dog if appropriate. If you advance to the level of recalling when playing, then it's best to wait for a pause in the play, otherwise, he may not even notice the whistle if he is in full flow.

Step 11: Continue to practice in other safe areas where you may want to let Fido off-leash. New areas should first be practised without the added distractions.

Note: The reason Fido comes to you when you blow the whistle is that he gets a treat and is also permitted to continue to play. This behaviour should be maintained by regularly blowing the whistle during off-leash time, giving a treat and allowing Fido to go and play again. On any occasion when you need to put Fido back on the leash, give him a few treats after attaching it. This will help to ensure that he is always happy to go back on the leash.

The advantage to using a whistle is that it is very distinctive. The disadvantage is that you may leave home without it. I always keep one on my keyring. However, the very same process can be done using a distinctive word or sound. I often use a WUB WUB sound, just because it's distinctive and can cut across other noises.

There are a few other things which we should consider in order to develop a really good recall. Receiving a regular treat for returning may lose its appeal. From the dog's perspective, they get a treat for returning, even if they didn't respond immediately. We still want to be giving them the treat, otherwise we could be encouraging them not to bother in future. There are training systems and arguments for not giving the treat for each and every recall. One being that we shape a faster return by only treating them for the quicker responses. A second is the idea that not knowing when the treat is going to come, makes the behaviour stronger, or more addictive, like gambling. However, there are also good arguments against such systems. On the whole, if I ask the dog to do something, I always try to say thank you with a treat, or game. So the way I improve the recall is by using varying rewards. I have a few different treats in my treat pouch. Maybe a few pieces of cubed cheese, some chicken shreds, and meat-based pate cubes. Not only this but I will often chuck the treat as the dog approaches, thereby increasing its value, because the dog now gets to chase it, and dogs usually love to chase treats in this way. I also use the occasional toy, or immediately play the 'find it' game (see enrichment chapter). It keeps things fresh and exciting.

Another thing to consider, especially with puppies, is that it's often (not always) immensely enjoyable to run over and play with other dogs. Monty loves nothing better than going to say hi to everyone and play is very much part of the natural development of dogs. So we have a natural urge which is immensely enjoyable, therefore reinforcing, meaning the behaviour is likely to occur again and again. But there's a problem! Not all dogs want to say hi, not all dog guardians want them to say hi. People with on-leash dogs often don't want your dog running over to them. Actually, you often never know; some are on-leash because of a poor recall, but others may be on-leash because of aggression, fear issues, injuries, arthritis etc. With this in mind, you should not allow your dog to run over to other dogs who are on-leash.

I'm usually pretty good at reading people from a distance; if they are showing any concerns, like putting their dog on-leash, changing direction, or bringing the dog closer to them, then I avoid them. But we can't always rely on how people behave. We are all slightly different and naturally, some people are on the wider margins of these differences so may not react or behave as we assume they will. I was recently walking Monty in a beautiful open countryside location which is commonly used by dog walkers. I was walking in the direction of a lady who had a yellow Labrador puppy of about the same age as Monty. She continued to walk towards me without any obvious concern. We got closer and closer to one another. I guess we were about the distance of a tennis court apart. Monty, being the friendly joyful soul that he is, trotted over to say hi to the yellow lab, who was also off-leash and showing happy and relaxed body language. However, when Monty got near, the lady grabbed her dog and put him on-leash – then set about trying to keep the dogs apart and looking at me like I was a monster. I shall never know why she did this as I saw no sign of fear or threat from either dog, but the point is, sometimes people don't act as you'd expect.

But here's the bigger problem; if Monty (or any other dog) always gets to go and say hi to other dogs and has a good time doing so, we are actually conditioning them to do just that. So what's going to happen? They are going to begin running over to every dog, or nearly every dog. That's not what we want. We need to be able to decide if the dog should go and say hello. We need to condition them to the fact that they do not automatically run over to every dog, especially on-leash dogs. With this in mind, it may be prudent to practice other things. Sometimes, if it's safe and appropriate, let them go and say hi, but at other times, when you see a dog in the distance, and before your dog gets too excited about going over there, play a game, throw some treats (not near other dogs as there may be dietary issues or resource guarding issues), run the other way calling them. Try to strike a balance so that they don't just assume they should run up to every dog. Another useful tactic is to play the 'wait' game; the release could be their cue to go and play. Another very useful aid is a long leash/line, see next chapter on walking together. The long line is a way of allowing freedom to wander and sniff, whilst preventing your pup getting themselves into too much trouble or learning to ignore you in favour of chasing after other dogs.

Checking in

If you watch for it, you may notice your dog checking in with you when you're walking them off-leash. The dog simply looks around to see where you are, reassuring themselves they are still with you. I like to reinforce this with a treat, which I also do when they run back to me without being called. Over time, this builds reinforcement of checking in and returning. It helps to keep a strong connection between us and the dog.

The environment can be a very stimulating place – all the new sights, sounds, and smells. We want the dog to enjoy these things, but we also benefit from maintaining a good relationship in these environments; we don't want the dog to forget we exist – they are not just walking, they are walking with their human. Some dogs are not such naturals at checking in. My West Highland Terrier, Daisy, did not check in naturally. There is almost certainly a genetic component to this. Terriers were selectively bred to be fierce and independent – I don't think Daisy received the 'fierce' memo, but she was certainly the most independent dog I ever raised. She did not seem to have a natural urge to check in with me – this was something I encouraged through calling her back to me for treats or to throw her toy. Making myself of interest in the environment encouraged her to check in more. I don't see this as competing with the environment – I'm not trying to be better than all the interesting things, I'm trying to add to them.

Walking Together

The problem with walking a dog on-leash is that it's completely unnatural. How is the dog to know we've attached ourselves to them purely to keep them safe? For most of their genetic history, they were not attached by a cord to anything or anyone. What do dogs make of this restriction to their desired movement? We will probably never know, but for many dogs, we can be fairly sure that it creates frustration.

There are, of course, good reasons for having the dog on-leash. The main consideration is one of safety. The last fifty years have seen a huge increase in cars on our roads. It's not safe for dogs to live in our towns and cities without being leashed. There are also other reasons a leash may be used. These include ensuring the dog doesn't become a nuisance to other people, complying with leash laws, and for training purposes. This unnatural, but often essential, attachment to us can also be frustrating for dog guardians. Pulling on-leash is one of the most common complaints I hear from people about their dog. In some cases, it can severely affect the relationship between human and dog, because the human often views 'pulling' as bad behaviour. It can also lead to dogs not getting daily walks, because the guardian either doesn't feel able to physically keep hold of the leash, or the daily walk becomes an unenjoyed chore, which the guardian increasingly skips.

The difference between human and dog in the tug-of-war which often occurs is that the human understands that the restriction is needed for safety. They understand that the objective is for the dog to walk without pulling us along. But we should be highly considerate of the fact that the dog is blind to these facts. They have no way of knowing that restrictive leash walking is for their safety, or to comply with local laws, or what the human's training objective might be. These are things created by humans – how could the dog possibly have any idea about our intentions? Whenever you are doing any on-leash walking/training, take a moment to consider what the experience is like for the dog, who doesn't possess the knowledge that you have. From the dog's perspective it probably feels a bit strange that we insist on reattaching the umbilical cord.

Many dog training books describe a kind of watered-down obedience heelwork system where you are told to reward the dog for looking up at you. The idea being that if you reinforce the behaviour of looking up at the handler, the dog will do this more often and, as they can't be looking up at you and pulling at the same time, it prevents pulling. Technically speaking, that is correct. But it doesn't make for a very good walk for the dog. Are we to believe that the best kind of walk our dog can have is one where they are walking along looking up at the handler? What about stopping to sniff and to look around, and to learn about their environment? The other factor, which is not usually taken into account, is that the average companion dog spends almost all of their time within the confines of their house and, usually, small garden or yard. They experience the inside of their home all day, every day. When the dog is taken for a walk – BOOM! – we just woke the brain to all those sights, sounds, and scents.

To a large extent pulling on the leash is caused by overstimulation as the dog is suddenly exposed to exciting stimuli. Add an overbearing guardian determined to maintain tight control of every move the dog makes and we have a surefire recipe for frustration.

My puppy, Monty, goes most places with me; I take him to work, where he's developing into a great office dog. He goes in and out of the house with me whenever I'm running errands in the car. He's in and out of the house quite a lot and involved in my daily activities, whilst also ensuring he gets lots of sleep (discussed later). He also has two off-leash opportunities in safe spaces, for example woodland, and a large open park near my town. I'm in a fortunate position in being able to take Monty with me to the office and out and about – it's much more difficult, or even impossible for others to do the same. However, the more a dog is going in and out of the home, the less likelihood of them becoming overstimulated by the event.

My recommendation for leashes, is that you purchase one of approximately 6 metres (19 feet), and a second one of approximately 2 metres. The long leash allows the dog to move further away for sniffing and is useful for practicing recall training. They are available in much longer lengths, but 6 metres allows for some puppy freedom whilst also being reasonably easy to handle without getting them tangled up. Long leashes should only be attached to well-fitted harnesses, not collars. I also recommend biothane leashes; they're waterproof so will not become soggy in wet weather. It may not matter so much for the short leash, but nobody wants to carry 6 metres of wet dog leash around.

These can only be fully utilised in open spaces, but they give the dog a little freedom to explore without the worry of not recalling. The main method is to hold the bulk of it (in loops) in one hand and control the length by letting it feed through your other hand. For walking near roads, or going to the vets etc, the shorter, 2 metre, leash will be your best option because the pup will not be going far from you. There is also the option of using a retractable leash; however, it is much easier for them to be pulled out of your hand, much harder to judge where the end is, and harder to slow the dog steadily – if you press the button to stop it unwinding, there's a very sudden stop for the dog. I think it's worth spending a little time getting used to handling a long line/leash, and avoiding the retractable leashes.

My general procedure for loose leash walking is allowing the dog to stop and sniff whenever they want. This helps to slow things down and allows the dog to use their brain as they decipher all those scents. If they pull, I stop walking forward. If dogs always move forward by pulling on a tight leash, then, from their perspective, that's how to move forward, so why would they not pull? Every time the lead goes tight, stop walking. If it helps, imagine a brick wall appearing in front of you. Just stop, and wait. Hold your hands against your body to secure the leash and prevent getting into a tug-of-war with the dog. The moment the tension slackens, continue to walk. This procedure does take time, and people are often impatient or inconsistent with it, but most dogs will learn to slow down as the leash tension increases. We can help the process by frequently giving food treats at our side or placing them by our foot. The dog then learns to watch out for this. We can also help by giving a food reward whenever the dog is walking nicely next to us. If this behaviour is frequently reinforced (with the treat), the dog is more likely to choose this position more often.

Try to remain relaxed, remember this is a difficult and very unnatural thing for the dog, who has no way of knowing what we are playing at. There are occasions when we do need to bring the dog in close at our side. Perhaps we're walking along a busy street. For this reason, I do teach dogs to do a slightly more formal heelwork walking at my side, but I don't expect this to be how the dog generally walks for the majority of the time. To expect the dog to maintain a heel position, focused on the human, for long durations is unrealistic and unnecessary for most companion dogs.

For bringing the dog in close to me I use heeling bursts. I simply have 10 treats in my hand. I let the dog sniff my hand and become interested. As I step forward, I give the dog a treat from my hand. I continue to treat for each step the dog follows my hand and stays by my side. This can be practiced in the garden or yard to begin with and then can be done whilst out walking. As the dog becomes proficient at this, you may move to taking two steps between treating, then three, then four and so on. If you are not getting the expected behaviour, you should move back to treating more frequently, and then building the distance again later.

Never release the treat if the dog is mouthing your hand, otherwise we will be inadvertently teaching them to mouth our hands. Over time you can move your hand higher, away from the dog's nose. Some people morph the position of the hand over time until it's flat against the person's hip. This becomes the signal for the dog to heel.

The other consideration is that if we have food in our hand every time we do the exercise, the smell of the food in the hand will become part of the signal which tells the dog to heel, meaning they become dependent on smelling it and may not respond when the hand is empty. For this reason it's good practice, once the dog is following your hand, to keep the food in a pocket. Doing this teaches the dog that they still get the treat, even though it's not in the hand. It's the difference between teaching them to follow food and teaching them to follow your hand. Both will work, but the latter is more useful. But remember, you still give them the treat. I only ever use this type of heelwork for short durations when I really need the dog close to me and focused.

For me, the most enjoyable type of walk is in a safe place away from traffic and for my dog to be off leash, enjoying free movement, but sadly that is not always possible.

300 Peck – or maybe 50 peck will do!

People often find loose leash training to be tedious. They find it difficult to be consistent, and this makes it even more difficult for the pup. There is a game you can play to make it fun; well maybe not fun, but at least a bit less tedious. 300 peck is an old training method; technically speaking it's a more of a reinforcement schedule than a training method, but that's splitting hairs. The idea of 300 peck is that it incrementally rewards the dog for continuing a behaviour for greater duration or distance. For walking, we don't need to worry about duration or distance; we can just count steps. It works like this:

The dog gets a treat for remaining at your side, without the leash going tight, for one step. If that's successful, the dog gets a treat for remaining at your side for two steps. If that's successful, the dog gets a treat for remaining at your side for 3 steps, and so on. It should look like this: one step, and treat – two steps, and treat – three steps, and treat. Each time you complete the required number of steps, you move up a level, adding another step to the requirement. If you are not successful you begin again at the very beginning – one step, and treat – two steps, and treat – three steps, and treat. The idea is that the animal (it was originally designed for pigeons) gets to restart at an easy level and gain lots of reinforcement, therefore building a strong association with the required behaviour. The original concept is to reach 300; however, it wasn't designed for loose leash walking; that would be asking too much of the dog and we would all lose count trying to get to 300. I think a more realistic target is 50 steps. If you can regularly reach 50, I'd stop there and just give a treat randomly. I'm aware one of my university lecturers may read this book, so I must point out that technically speaking, there is no such thing as random – so give a treat 'now and again' instead.

Please remember that you and the dog are a team. Training isn't about trying to force compliance on them. Training isn't about getting them to do it – it's about so much more than that. It's about our relationship – it's about being fair – it's about allowing them to enjoy life. We are not trying to get the dog to walk for miles at our side, looking up at us – we're building relationships, not robots.

A Time for Silence

The unique thing about humans is our rather elaborate language system. The Oxford English dictionary lists over 171,000 words in current usage. They're a fabulous way of communicating, of telling stories, of teaching, and of learning. We take language for granted, but I still find it amazing that I can sit in my house, and the words I write (or speak) can teach people, on the other side of the planet, about how to raise a puppy. However, when it comes to communicating with our dogs, our strong reliance on language can get in the way. I'm not against talking to our dogs, feel free to chatter away (I often do), just as long as you're not expecting too much from the dog in return.

The problem comes when we insist on giving verbal instructions that the dog has no way of understanding. We can associate words with behaviours that we want from the dog (known as adding verbal cues), without any trouble, if we do it correctly. However, we are such a vocal species that we often expect the dog to know what we're saying. Phrases like, leave that alone, come down the stairs, don't do that, get off my shoes, lie down, drop the ball, etc. Because we are so reliant on vocal language, without thinking about it, we assume the dog is disobeying or ignoring us, when actually, they very often have no clue what we're saying. When I'm working on training a new behaviour, I usually do it in silence. This is how pups best learn because it relies on us concentrating on our own body language and prevents us repeating words the dog does not yet understand, and it helps us to avoid blaming the puppy for our own errors. It's far more peaceful and relies more on the connection between you and the dog rather than using verbal language, which, with the best will in the world, is a very one-sided event. There is very little that a deaf dog cannot learn just as easily as a hearing dog; in fact, they often excel because people are not expecting them to understand verbal language.

The process of training most behaviours we want from a dog is to work out a way of getting them to do the thing (or a tiny part of the thing, to begin with) and once we are happy that they can do it, we can add a cue. For example, imagine we wanted to train the dog to place their front paws on a cushion; I might begin by having a piece of food in my hand and getting them to follow it onto the cushion, then releasing the food. This process is known as luring. When they are proficient at doing this, I might use my hand to lure them, but without any food inside. This prevents them becoming dependent on seeing or smelling the food before participating. They still get rewarded with a piece of food (reinforcement), but it's produced from elsewhere – not the luring hand. Then, when they are proficient, I might start to reduce my hand movement; instead of being in front of their nose I might move it an inch away, then another inch away. I can also reduce the amount of hand movement over time until I'm doing no more than pointing towards the cushion. The dog still gets a treat for placing their feet on the cushion. This is an example of how training can be done without uttering a word to the dog. Now, if you want to, you can add a verbal cue. Just before pointing at the cushion, you might say 'feet up' then point. The dog learns to associate the word 'feet up' with the behaviour and before long you will be able to stop pointing and just give the verbal cue 'feet up'. The cushion can then be put in other places to teach the dog to put their feet up wherever you ask. The cushion can also be withdrawn so the dog puts their feet up on things without its presence. My book, *Dog Training & Behaviour: a guide for everyone,* has much more on the technical aspects of training if you're interested in taking it further, but the point here is that it is often better to try and work on behaviours without speaking. Actually, it's a lovely break from how we communicate with humans, and I find it rather therapeutic.

Agency

The daily challenges which face wild animals are vast; for example, competing with other animals for food, water, and mates, while avoiding predation. These life skills develop as the animal's genetics, and developing brain, are exposed to different real-life experiences. If the challenges become too great, the animal may not survive, for example, forest fires, and the ever-decreasing natural habitat. However, captive animals, including our companion dogs, may face no challenges at all. Indeed, they may have very few choices in life. Very often the human makes all decisions, from what and when to eat, to where and when to walk – even the ability to stop and sniff is at the mercy of the human.

Agency is the ability of an individual to interact with their environment of their own volition in ways that promote their experience and skill set. A real-life example of how a lack of agency affects the pup's development is this: pups are removed from their littermates and, very often, do not get further opportunities to play with dogs for a considerable amount of time. In many cases, they don't see other dogs until they've had their inoculations, then may live in an area with strict leash laws, or have guardians who severely limit socialisation experiences – often to protect the puppy. These restrictions are understandable, but from a dog's perspective, their natural development and learning of dog-to-dog social skills has been hampered through lack of agency. Ironically, we do this, but then blame the dog when they are overstimulated by the sight of other dogs. We cannot solve all the imperfections of modern life, but we should have a little empathy and humility – the majority of dog behaviour problems are a side effect of human behaviour.

When I visited the zoo as a child, many years ago, the enclosures had very little in them, other than the animals. They were just large cages with very little for the animal to do. In such conditions animals still choose to interact with their environment, but their agency is severely restricted, preventing a reasonable degree of exploration, development opportunities, social play, or behavioural diversity. These barren environments led to behavioural issues and poor mental wellbeing. Evolution has equipped animals with a brain which is primed for learning; this allows them to develop into masters of their environment. The more restrictive the environment, the fewer opportunities there are for them to gain this mastery. You cannot learn life skills without experiencing life.

A lack of agency and the stunted development of life skills increases the likelihood of anxiety and fear – not only does the animal lack experience, they lack choice and will find coping with environmental changes more difficult. Consider how our companion dogs are restricted. Many restrictions are essential for safety and to comply with regional laws, but where it is possible and safe, we should promote agency. This is not about exposing them to everything and letting them get on with learning. If an experience is too boring the dog may not engage at all, yet if it seems too risky, we might see the dog avoid interaction through fear. For example, the puppy may ignore a small puddle, and be terrified of a fast-flowing river, but a shallow stream may be just right to allow them to take a small degree of risk, pushing through their uncertainty, and learning as they splash around. We need to show them life's streams.

Opportunities to Increase Agency

Sniffing

Animals are primed to pay attention to novel stimuli. In the wild, this pays by providing opportunities to gain valuable resources, or by avoiding danger. Watch your dog in the home and you will probably not notice too much sniffing; the odours are predictable and of no real interest. Compare this to how much time the dog spends sniffing outside of the home. They very clearly have a need to detect who's been around. This behaviour is often seen by guardians as bothersome because they want to get on with walking, but it is actually an opportunity to give the dog back some agency. As long as it is safe to do so, let the dog lead you for a change; walk where they want to sniff and see where it takes you.

Play

Play helps young animals, not only to develop fine motor skills and agility, but also emotional regulation. It also plays an important role in building bonds with dogs and humans. Dogs tend to vary in playstyles.

Some seem to enjoy a little rough and tumble with their human, while others prefer to chase and tug. We should take the time to consider the dog's perspective – are they enjoying it as much as we think? Play for a very short time, perhaps five seconds, and see if your puppy is keen to re-engage. Play, training, and everything else, is not something we do *to* dogs, it is something we do *with* dogs. If it's possible for you, it's also a very good idea to facilitate dog-to-dog play with suitable, socially well adjusted, playmates.

Food Enrichment Toys

Contrafreeloading is a behaviour whereby, when given a choice between obtaining food from a bowl or from a food dispenser, requiring effort, the animal chooses the food dispenser. You might expect animals to always select the easiest option, but that doesn't account for their need to practice skills and engage their brain. Enrichment feeding can be an excellent way of engaging the brain and promoting agency. The idea is that some of their daily food allowance is stuffed into food enrichment toys, for example, *Kong Classic, West Paw Tux, West Paw Toppl*, and *K9 Connectables*. As with many things in the dog world, this can be controversial. Some people believe it is unkind to make the dog work for their food. However, it is not about force, it is about giving the dog opportunities to engage their brain and widen behavioural skill sets and promote mental wellbeing. We must look for the sweet spot – not scary or frustrating, not boring, – interesting and engaging. A food enrichment toy could easily become frustrating for a young puppy, who lacks the concentration of a mature dog. To begin with, I place food inside very loosely so that it falls out easily. Over time, this can be compacted. At six months of age, Monty now has a stuffed food toy while I'm eating my own dinner, but this is only about 10% of his daily food allowance. Over time, this will likely increase to 50% of his food.

Safety

Another consideration in our quest to promote agency is the dog's feeling of safety. All animals have an innate need for safety. If animals did not seek safety, they would not live long enough to pass on their genes to future generations. This doesn't mean they are always able to make wise choices in a world dominated by humans; for example, they may have poor judgement when it comes to road safety. Agency allows wild animals to flee and seek refuge if they perceive a threat, but what about domesticated species, like our companion dog? If they do not feel safe, they can't pack up their things and use agency to relocate. Imagine a home where the dog is repeatedly chastised, yelled at, or even physically punished. Do they feel safe? Or would they choose another home? What kind of home would you choose for yourself? Dogs are captive, but we don't have to tell them this! We can be the home and the guardian they would choose.

Agency is very often overlooked as a principle of animal behaviour. Fundamentally, agency is about giving animals some degree of control over their environment. Obviously, this is limited – it's always our responsibility to keep them safe. However, when it comes to dogs, we've been somewhat brainwashed into thinking they must obey our every wish. This mindset has spoiled many budding dog/human relationships and we've often been encouraged to force the dog to comply. I imagine there are many dog trainers reading this and sneering, but the best way to get a dog to do anything is to give them a fair choice – we should allow them to say no. It may seem paradoxical to allow the dog to say 'no, I don't want to do that', because, obviously, if we are training them a behaviour, we want them to do it. However, imagine the puppy who wriggles and scratches when they're picked up. Forcing the dog to submit to our will is likely to lead to them avoiding being picked up in the future and possibly becoming aggressive when we (or somebody else) try to do so. However, if we put the puppy down when they first begin to wriggle, they may learn that they can get down at any time with a slight wriggle. Because they can now choose to get down, they're more likely to enjoy being picked up

Enrichment (enjoying puppyhood)

I'm quite well known for my interest in enrichment. Whenever I do a dog behaviour talk, on any area of behaviour, it always comes around to people asking me about enrichment. This is largely because my first book was on the subject, and I started the first ever Facebook group specifically for canine enrichment, which, at the time of writing, stands at half a million members. Animal enrichment began in zoos (Hal Markowitz being one of the main pioneers) as a way of improving the welfare of their animals. Essentially, enrichment is the process of encouraging/facilitating natural behaviour – these are behaviour patterns that the animal might do if they were not prevented from doing so by captivity. They allow the animal to use their fantastic brains, thereby improving mental welfare. I don't think any amount of enrichment can replace natural living so there remain ethical questions about the existence of zoos, but while they do exist, it's far better that they consider the animals' mental welfare.

What we never seem to consider is that our dogs are also captive animals – they are domesticated, which means they've 'evolved' towards fitting in with human needs, but nevertheless, they are very much captive and under our tight control. Dogs were selectively bred into over 1,000 different breeds (not all still in existence) for working roles in human societies. The majority of these working roles no longer exist; for example, only a tiny percentage of Border Collies will ever herd sheep. Most dogs (other than free-roaming dogs, which are prolific in some parts of the world) live as companions to their human families. We love dogs so much that we still keep them around long after their value as working dogs has dried up. The problem is that their fantastic brain no longer has a job to do. That's fine, you might think, we don't need them to do any jobs! However, good mental wellbeing relies on mental stimulation. Without positive mental stimulation, animals may become depressive or develop harmful or problematic behaviours as they try to relieve the stress. The phenomenon of stereotypies (repetitive behaviour which serves no obvious function) in animals is widely known in the world of animal behaviour science and is often attributed to inadequate mental stimulation. Our companion dogs are known to improve our mental wellbeing; I contend that we owe it to them to look after their mental wellbeing in return.

My enrichment book was written with adult dogs in mind. The life of a young puppy is already quite full of activities. They're usually full of enthusiasm and keen to investigate the world. They are being socialised and habituated to their new life, and they tend to get a lot of attention in these early days. With this in mind, I often do not think of puppy activities as enrichment; nor do I think about it as training. Raising a puppy is more about the pup's development and building a relationship with the world and with their human. Recently, I was asked how I was training Monty, 'I'm not training' I said 'I'm relationshipping.' They were a little puzzled, mainly because I'd just made up a verb, but language is ever evolving and 'relationshipping' is my contribution.

The problem I often see is that people are keen to train the pup to do things – almost immediately we are putting pressure on them to be a certain way and do a certain thing. If it doesn't go to plan, we're disappointed. What we forget, amidst the hard work of puppy raising, is to have some fun and to let the puppy have some fun. Just as a child should enjoy childhood, a puppy should enjoy puppyhood.

There are many ways of having fun and building a good relationship. It's not about buying expensive toys. Your greatest asset is you. Have lots of fun together – here's a few simple things to do together:

Cardboard boxes

Cardboard boxes can be great fun for puppies to play with and gain confidence. Some caution is needed as some boxes have staples in them, while others have glue. The boxes shouldn't be left with the puppy, and they are not for the pup to chew. However, great fun can be had with a few cardboard boxes turned sideways. Throw some toys and treats inside them and let the pup have fun investigating.

Run away

Get your pups attention, then run away so the pup chases you. When they catch you, play a little game of gentle tug with a toy, or give them a treat. I don't recommend this on shiny floors, they are not good for dogs or people to run on. This may be a game best reserved for the garden or on carpet.

Plastic cups

Place a treat under a plastic cup. As soon as the puppy nudges it with their nose or foot, lift up the cup and let them have the treat. When they get the hang of it, use two cups but only place a treat under one. Next step is to place the treat and mix up the cups, as soon as pupster indicates a cup, raise it up. You can later increase to three cups.

Hide and seek

Hide, just out of sight, then call the puppy to find you. Remember to make it super easy to begin with. We are never trying to outsmart the pup or make it too difficult or cause stress. It should be fun and it's our job to ensure the pup always wins.

Hand touch

Hold out your hand so the palm is pointing towards the dog, when they give a little sniff, say 'yes' and give a treat. Later this simple little game can be used in all sorts of ways, from a silent recall to a way of guiding the puppy onto the scales at the veterinarians. If pupster doesn't sniff your hand, rub a little cheese on there to get him started.

Muffin tin

Place pieces of his food in muffin tin compartments and cover the compartments with toys and balls.

Obstacle course

Make an obstacle course for him to walk over. Don't make it difficult, it's about building confidence of walking over different items. Perhaps start with a few cushions on the floor, then perhaps the cushions followed by a large book, then maybe add a rolled-up mat, so they are all in a row, then maybe a dining chair for him to walk underneath. Joints are still forming during puppyhood so don't encourage jumping. Pups do jump around a lot but we shouldn't add to it. To begin with you will need some treats and you will get the pup to follow your hand over the course. Start by treating for every obstacle and, when they are more confident, treat halfway and again at the end. If you are doing this in the garden/yard you could even lay a ladder flat on the floor as part of the course.

Scatter feeding

Take a handful of their food and scatter it across the floor, like you're feeding chickens. Just enjoy watching them find every piece.

Sniffing (sniffari)

When you take them out on a leash, let them sniff. So many people have the idea that the dog should walk at their side, and they get annoyed when the pupster wants to keep stopping for a sniff. Remind yourself that they are just a baby investigating the world and, to a dog, scent is very much their world. Studies by Duranton and Horowitz (2019) found that daily olfactory enrichment improved the emotional wellbeing of dogs and made them more optimistic. I was so intrigued by their work, it formed the basis of my own research during my MSc degree.

Flick

Take a piece of food and simply flick it across the floor for your pup to chase and eat.

Treasure hunt

Hide treats around the house and send the dog to find them. This game brings together the dog's superb scenting ability with the seeking system. The thrill of the chase is on! It's quite easy to teach a dog to go searching.

Step 1: Let the pup see you put a treat down on the floor and allow him to get it. Maybe saying 'search' as he begins. He doesn't know what the word means yet, but as long as it comes just before he moves towards the treat, he'll soon learn that this word means, look for treats. It's easier if the dog already knows how to 'wait' so you can ask for a wait before placing the treat, but it's not essential.

Step 2: When he's been happily doing step 1 for a few days, start putting the treat where he can't actually see it, but he can see where you are putting it. For example, you could have a cushion on the floor and place a treat just to the far side of the cushion. After a few days of this you will be ready for step 3.

Step 3: Start to place the treat at times he can't see you doing it. Then give the cue word - 'search.'

Step 4: Very slowly make the game more challenging by finding new places to hide the food. It should always be where he can access it. Never trick or tease him. If you want to hide treats in more than one place, start at the beginning again and let him see there is more than one location with treats. Maybe use two or three cushions on the floor and have treats behind each. When you know all the treats have been found, you could say 'all done' and give another piece of food. They soon learn that no more are to be found and they can relax. Young pups will not have great concentration levels so it's best to keep the game very simple. When he reaches about six months, you'll find that his concentration increases, and he'll be able to focus on finding the scent for longer.

Trail

Tie a sausage to a piece of string and drag it across your garden/yard. Leave a treat at the end of the trail. Show the puppy where the trail begins and see if they can follow the scent trail to find the treat. You can start this really easily by making the trail really short or dropping treats part way along.

Find It

My favourite game of all time is to teach the puppy to find an item. I would suggest beginning this game from around five months of age.

You could use any soft dog toy for this, I'm currently using a small teddy bear (about six inches tall), designed for dogs. You'll also need to purchase a tub of dried catnip.

Step 1: Place some catnip in an airtight container (enough to cover the bottom). Place kitchen roll (paper towel) over the catnip and place your dog toy on top of the kitchen roll, replace the lid and leave overnight. The toy will absorb the odour of the catnip and this provides a distinctive scent for the dog to find.

Step 2: Using the toy, play fetch with your dog, throwing it just a short distance. If your dog doesn't fetch things back to you, no worries, you can just let him chase and grab the toy. To get it back, have another toy to throw or switch to some scatter feeding with a few treats. Be careful not to chuck the toy again until the dog has well and truly stopped eating for at least 10 seconds. If the dog is reliably fetching or at least chasing and picking up the item, you can tell him to 'Find It' whenever you throw the toy. This will become the dog's signal to go and look for the item later in the process.

Step 3: Place the toy, instead of throwing it, and encourage the dog to 'Find It'. Reward with another toy, game or food.

Step 4: Start putting the toy just out of sight but allow him to see where you put it (maybe in an open box).

Step 5: Place it in easy to find places but without him seeing where you put it.

Step 6: Increase the difficulty by placing the toy in more challenging places around the house or garden and telling him to 'Find it'.

If he sees you get the container, he will certainly know that the game is on so will not be too dependent on the 'Find it' signal. It is nice to have the signal (cue) if you advance to hiding the toy without his knowledge.

Always ensure the dog is competent and keen at each step and always play fair. Don't ever place it where he can't reasonably access it. This is extremely good brain exercise. You can see the concentration and focus as the dog uses scent, not just casually, but purposefully, to find a particular object. This is a dog truly being a dog.

Settle

One of the downsides to enrichment is that some people take it to extremes. Puppies (and adult dogs) usually require a lot of down time. At 8 weeks of age the pup will probably sleep for around 19 hours per day and by adulthood will sleep around 14 hours per day. Their sleep is not in one block, like our own, but takes the form of many separate sleeps over a 24-hour period (polyphasic). People sometimes get the idea that the puppy, or dog, always needs to be doing something or being entertained. As soon as the human moves, the dog is up and alert and watching for what game you're going to play, or what adventure you're both going on. This isn't always going to be what we want, and it may hinder the dog's ability to just relax and get their rest.

There are a few things we can do which will help the dog's ability to remain relaxed, or even to relax after an activity. To begin with, think about all the times your puppy gets a reward (or reinforcer); it's almost always when they are active. What we want to do is teach them that, (1) they don't always need to be doing things to get the good stuff, and (2) relaxation brings the good stuff to them. Throughout the day, when you see them relaxed, give a small treat. To begin with this works best if you are sitting near them rather than needing to approach and walk away, which may be more stimulating. After a few weeks of doing this, maybe 3 or 4 times per day, begin giving the treat as you walk past them, as long as they are relaxed. You do not need to stop treating when you are sitting next to them, you can just do a little of both. To begin with, the treat may bring them out of their relaxed state but, over time, they will learn that there's nothing too exciting going on and there are no more treats coming. This will work best if you have easy access to the treats, so maybe have a few pots stashed around the home or keep them in your pocket. It's probably a good idea for the treats not to be too exciting, so fresh chicken is probably out of the question.

Over time this exercise will help them remain relaxed, but it can also be used to induce a relaxed state. For this it is best to have a small, easily transported, mat. Place the mat where they often relax, maybe on their bed or on the sofa. The mat can then be used in other places to make it more likely that they will lie down and relax. Many protocols for training this involve first training the dog to lie down when asked, then using the 'lie down' cue to get them to lie down on the mat. Actually, what often happens is that the dog gets a treat (reinforcement) for lying down or lying down and staying in that position, rather than being relaxed. I don't usually give a verbal cue; I guess I don't really believe you can tell somebody (or your dog) to relax.

How often have you been told to relax? It's not so easy is it? What we need to do is merely invite them to relax and make that the most likely outcome. With Monty, we couldn't decide if we were going to permit him onto the sofa. This is not something our previous dogs have ever done. With my previous Labrador, Mr B, I sat on the floor with him so much that he just never attempted to get on the sofa, not once. Monty on the other hand, decided from day one that it seemed like a pretty good spot to be. The issue was that we wanted our guests to be able to sit on the sofa without getting an enthusiastic Labrador in their face. There are other considerations too, such as the possibility of him jumping up unexpectedly as somebody is drinking a hot drink. The answer was to use a folded blanket (or throw). I placed the blanket on one half of the sofa; the half where Monty usually chose to settle. He soon got accustomed to settling in that spot. Occasionally I would place it on the other sofa and invite him up by patting it. If he ever got on the sofa without the blanket in place, I simply lured him off, and patted the blanket to invite him onto that section. Not only did this allow us to choose where on the sofa Monty would lie, it produced a very good indicator of relaxation. I don't need to ask him to lie down, I simply tap the blanket and he generally chooses to lie on it and relax.

Over time, the blanket, rug, or whatever you are using, can be moved to other areas in order to invite the dog to relax on it. The mat can even be taken away because once the dog is very used to relaxing when you tap the mat, you can transfer this to tapping similar mats, then less similar areas, maybe a large pillow or a rug. It can then be transferred to simply tapping the floor as an indicator to settle down. You should remember two things, (1) to quietly reward them (every so often) when they are settled, and (2) it is not an order you are giving; you are simply inviting them to settle in the spot you just tapped. This is not the same as teaching a down-stay; in a down-stay the dog is likely to be alert and waiting for what's going to happen next. That's not what we are trying to achieve here – we are just inviting the dog to settle.

Preventing Separation Anxiety

In my previous book, *Dog Training and Behaviour: a guide for everyone*, I discuss, at length, how to treat separation anxiety. Here the emphasis is on preventing the development of separation anxiety in the first place. Separation distress is often a heart-breaking and difficult problem to solve. It basically consists of the dog becoming desperately anxious, and becoming panicked, when isolated from humans. Sometimes it relates to a particular member of the family the dog is hyper attached to. The main reason it is difficult to fix is that it requires the dog not to be left alone for long periods during the behaviour modification process, or in other words, they cannot learn that being alone feels okay, if they are left alone for periods of time which continually triggers the anxiety. If they could, separation anxiety wouldn't exist.

This is difficult for people to achieve because they may have to go to work and leave the dog. Apart from the fact that separation related distress is obviously hard on the dog, it can be hard on the dog's guardian too because it may result in damage to the home as the dog tries to escape or relieve the stress.

Dogs are not robots or computers, so there are never any guarantees. We could provide identical environments and early experiences for two different dogs – one may develop separation anxiety while the other does not – brains are extremely complex things.

However, we can still stack the deck in our favour. We can do all we can to ensure that separation never becomes stressful in the first place. In the words of Benjamin Franklin (1736) 'an ounce of prevention is worth a pound of cure.'

When we take on a puppy, we are, to a large extent, becoming the puppy's parent figure. We are their place of safety, and separation from that safety can be extremely distressing. Ideally, we would never leave the pup and the ability to be alone would develop naturally as the pup grows and starts to develop more independence. But, as I often have to remind myself, we don't live in an ideal world. The majority of us live in quite small properties and we have a responsibility to keep the dog safe, which may hinder the development of independence. Added to this, a great number of people have no choice but to leave the dog home alone, so they can go and earn a living.

I was contacted recently by somebody who said their puppy had separation anxiety and the neighbours were complaining that the puppy was making a lot of noise during the day. On further investigation it transpired that the 10-week-old pup was being left home alone for 10 hours per day. They wanted me to advise on what enrichment they could give to the dog that would last for 10 hours. There is no such thing. There is no toy or activity that will enrich the pup's life, or keep them occupied, happy, or content for 10 hours. What the puppy needs is human interaction and to feel safe with their protector. It's easy to be judgemental, but the owner had simply not considered what a young puppy actually needs. They were not mean, or uncaring; it just hadn't occurred to them that, from the pup's perspective, they'd just gone from living with their mother and littermates, and all the interaction and joy that brings, to being totally alone all day, day after day. A puppy simply cannot develop normally under these conditions. It's very easy to rush into the decision to get a puppy, but it is very common that people don't evaluate the puppy's needs.

If you need to leave the pup at home while you work, I strongly suggest taking as much leave as possible to coincide with getting your puppy. If there are other adults in the house you may be able to work this between you to give the pup more time before being left. Other considerations, for when you return to work, are puppy sitters, or daycare, but these can be expensive and you need to ensure the pup will be happy. If you are friendly with your neighbours, they may enjoy puppy sitting for you, or maybe you have a relative who's home during the day who would like the company. These are not ideal solutions. Ideally, we want to be doing all the puppy raising, building a bond and ensuring consistency, but it is far better than leaving a young pup alone.

If you're lucky enough not to have to leave your dog, it's still important to teach them to feel safe when left. The day will come when you need to go out and can't take the dog with you. Many people took the opportunity to get puppies during the covid crisis that engulfed the world. Many were working from home and could spend all day with their dog. However, as life began to go back to normal, many people, once again, had to return to the office. There was a huge rise in reported cases of separation anxiety during this time. It was great that the pups were raised with lots of time with their human, but many of them had never learned that being alone was fine.

As with all things in dog training and development, your task is to make it easy for the dog to succeed. It's not really about the dog doing what you tell them, at least, not from the dog's perspective it isn't. From the dog's perspective, they are just doing what they think is the right thing to do. If we want the dog to do something, it's prudent (and fun) to let them think it was their idea.

If I want the puppy to learn to be alone, I make it very easy for them. This might start with me just stepping outside of the room and immediately coming back in. I don't close the door; it is their choice what they want to do. I do this very often, so Monty learns that he doesn't have to constantly follow me around, it's no big deal if I step out of sight. This is something that can be increased over time. Maybe extending the period you are out of sight by a second or two each day. Another cunning plan is to give him his food, then wander in and out of the room. At this stage I keep coming back in, I want to avoid anxiety. If I stayed outside of the room, although he would probably stay and eat, he would probably learn to eat faster and faster and then run to find me – that's not what we want. I practice this in different rooms of the house. These games (it's best to think of them that way) can be transferred to the garden/yard (if you have one) so you are able to step into the house with puppy in the garden, or step into the garden with puppy in the house. You are simply building up confidence of being alone. It's also a good idea to leave the puppy with a friend for a second or two and build this time up slowly. This is slowly progressed into leaving the house, literally for a second and returning. You might do this 20 times per day. What the puppy is learning is that it's no big deal, in fact it's quite boring. Again, this should be slowly increased over many weeks or months (if possible), until pup is quite happy being left.

If you are using a crate, this could also be very useful. You could give puppy something nice in there while you come and go, so that being left is no big deal. You have the added benefit of knowing that the puppy is safe and can't damage anything. I also have dog beds in different areas of the house. This way Monty can (and does) choose to go into another room by himself and have a sleep. If the pup is always shut in a room with you, they'll find it difficult to develop independence.

However, even with these foundations in place, we must consider the pup's needs. Leaving pups for extended periods is best avoided if possible. At six months of age, I leave Monty for approximately 20 minutes. I'm extremely fortunate, that I do not need to leave him home alone; I only do this to prepare him for future events. Many readers will have a need to leave their dogs for longer and at an earlier age. My previous Lab (my beloved Mr B) was left for up to 3 hours at a time by 6 months of age. It's not ideal, a young developing brain needs stimulation and social companionship but, as I've said previously, we do not live in ideal circumstances. Mr B also had the benefit of another dog in the house, which can be a great help, but it's in no way a replacement for their human. Getting a second dog to help a dog who's already suffering separation anxiety can easily result in having two dogs with separation anxiety.

It can be very difficult to juggle all the demands of modern life, and now I'm suggesting we shouldn't leave our pups for long periods. This is not written to shame anyone, we can all only do our best, and giving up your job to stay home isn't an option for most people. However, we must do whatever we can to limit home alone time, especially for young pups.

Other considerations for reducing the risk of separation anxiety include ensuring the dog's other needs are being met. Are they getting socialisation experiences and gaining confidence? If they are stressed in other areas of life, they may be more likely to suffer separation anxiety. Are they getting sufficient mental stimulation and enrichment? Enrichment activities can improve confidence and development, and olfactory enrichment is known to improve mental wellbeing (affective state) and optimism. When we are considering how to help the dog, it's usually best to look at the bigger picture, factoring in their whole wellbeing.

Fireworks

One of the things that dogs often struggle with is the sound of fireworks. It's hardly surprising. How are they to make sense of these mini explosions going off from all directions? In many cases, the dog is absolutely terrified and it's a heart-breaking sight. There are a few things we can do to try and ensure this fear doesn't develop. The first thing is that we can play firework noises each day while the puppy is young. This can be done with smart phone apps or *YouTube* recordings. Another method is to use a smart speaker, such as *Alexa*, to play firework sounds. More recently, I've begun using taiko drum recordings as they make a very good bass noise, similar to loud fireworks.

The recordings should be played at a very low volume (so you can barely hear it) and steadily increased over a month or two. We don't even want the puppy to notice them; they are just an insignificant background noise. In the UK, we have fireworks on and around November 5th; the US have fireworks at July 4th and the majority of countries have fireworks at New Year, as well as their own special celebratory days.

I live in the UK and my new puppy, Monty, was born on 27th September. This means he was 5.5 weeks of age when November 5th fireworks were occurring. It also means he was coming to the end of the primary socialisation period and beginning the secondary socialisation period (roughly, as these periods are not exact). To hear fireworks at this time, while still in the safety of his litter is likely to be a very good thing.

Added benefits included the fact that he was born in the countryside near to a small village; he therefore heard fireworks in the distance but not loud enough to cause any startle response. He also began life in the same room as a noisy washing machine and heard plenty of bangs and clangs around the farm. This early experience has made for a very good start in life, and he is unbothered by most sounds.

Often, new puppy parents will try to keep everything quiet so they don't frighten the puppy; the problem with this is that the pup needs to live in the real world and be unbothered by noise, as much as possible. I don't recommend tiptoeing around the house; I recommend gently introducing them to various noises at a low level and increasing it over time, as long as the puppy is not showing any concern. If they are showing concern, we may need to reduce the intensity back down to a level where they are unbothered and work our way back up again. This doesn't occur over night; it should be a process built up over a few months.

There is a popular belief that we should not comfort our dogs if they are afraid of fireworks. The thinking is that comforting will act as reinforcement for the fear and so make it more likely to occur. However, fear cannot be reinforced in the same way behaviour is reinforced, because fear is not a behaviour, it is an emotion.

Imagine, as a child, being afraid of thunder. You're sitting watching the TV one evening when there's a huge thunderstorm. Your heart fills with dread and you run to your mum for comfort. Your mum, understanding your fear, gives you a hug and tells you that everything's going to be okay; she is sure the storm will soon pass; she sits with you until it does.

Would that make you more likely to be afraid, or would it feel a little better knowing you're with your mum? Most of us would feel less afraid knowing we can seek comfort. Being afraid isn't an operant behaviour. A dog can choose to sit in order to get a treat, but they cannot choose to be afraid in order to get that treat.

Resource guarding

It's not uncommon for dogs to resource guard, either their food or particular items. Resource guarding is quite natural, even humans resource guard. Consider how many locks there are in the world; there are billions! The purpose of locks is to protect our things; locks are clearly a form of human resource guarding. The dog doesn't have the luxury of locks and can only use what is available to them – behaviour. Resource guarding has many different levels; for example, many dogs, when given a treat to chew, will carry that item away to a quiet spot away from people and/or other dogs. This could be considered as a low level of resource guarding because the function of carrying the item away is probably to protect that item and keep it to themselves. I'm quite happy for my dogs to do this. As the level of resource guarding increases, you may see them eating an item quickly, remaining very still, showing the whites of their eyes (whale eye), growling, snarling, air snapping, or biting.

We usually view resource guarding as bad behaviour, but from the dog's perspective, resource guarding is a means of asking people, or other dogs, to back off. The dog fears losing their precious resource and is trying to warn others. We often consider this to be an act of aggression, but the behaviour usually functions to avoid physical conflict by warning others about the dog's discomfort with their proximity. However, resource guarding can become very dangerous and we must remain aware of this, especially around vulnerable people, such as children and the elderly.

Resource guarding is not only seen in adult dogs; we may notice it more easily in adult dogs because it becomes more dangerous but often it may develop in puppyhood. The problem is, with puppies we may see it as cute and fail to do anything about it. The traditional advice used to be that you should be able to take anything away from your dog. However, what this teaches the dog is that you're going to take their things away. This may make the resource guarding worse, or it may be that they reluctantly allow their main carer to take things but they still find it threatening when approached. Imagine a child walking too close to them! It could end disastrously. The focus on preventing resource guarding should be the idea that we are no threat to them. When my pups (or adult dogs) are eating, I never take their food away, and I never let them think I will. Instead, when they have something tasty, like a beef tendon to chew on, I may throw them a piece of chicken. Over time they associate me going anywhere near them, with getting an extra treat, not with losing what they have. Safety must always come first; as responsible dog guardians we have a moral and a legal duty to ensure the safety of everyone our dog may come into contact with. Never take any chances. The safety of young children is paramount and they should always be supervised around dogs. A dog's reaction to a child approaching their food may be more severe than an adult approaching. We also have a duty to teach children to respect the dog and allow them peace while eating.

The *leave it/drop it* and the *swap it/drop it* exercises (in this book) will also help the dog learn from puppyhood that leaving things can be fun – this is useful when they pick up something dangerous, or maybe not dangerous, but disgusting. If you have multiple dogs, I like to feed them in separate rooms so they can eat without worrying about what the other dog is doing.

Twenty Things Your Pup Desperately Wants to Tell You

1: I'm always watching, picking up on your behaviour, connecting all the dots and making associations. Without any purposeful training, I will learn who you are and what you're about. Please learn who I am.

2: I don't need an authoritarian pack leader, I need an advocate and a guide.

3: Humans often expect far too much. I have a mental capacity equivalent to a 2-year-old child – nurture me.

4: Just like you, I have fears and anxieties.

5: If you want to improve behaviour, start with your own (damn right dogs can be sassy).

6: I'm not a machine, I have emotions.

7: Let's enrich each other's life.

8: I love hanging out with you.

9: You never have to hurt me to show me the way.

10: I'm not stubborn – more likely I'm lacking understanding or motivation.

11: I don't yank your neck – please don't yank mine.

12: Humans have been selectively breeding us for thousands of years – we're not trying to dominate you.

13: I'm sorry if I'm a bit exuberant at times – it's difficult growing up at this speed.

14: I'm a scent detector with a life support system – please let me sniff.

15: I might not be able to tell you when I'm in pain – watch for any changes in my behaviour.

16: I don't know what bad behaviour is – I'm just doing what seems most appropriate.

17: Put your phone down and make time for me.

18: Don't tell me I'm adopted – I refuse to believe it.

19: I won't be here long enough – love me today.

20: I love you.

The Final Word

On the 27th of April 2022, I lost my beloved Labrador, Mr B. He was nine years of age and cancer had robbed us of the years we had left together. I adored Mr B., and I think the feeling was mutual. I'm sorry, but this day will come for you too – this day comes for us all. It is, beyond doubt, the hardest thing about loving dogs. I didn't get everything right, but when I look back, my memories are filled with the good things we did together. I remember walking along riverbanks, through woodlands, and across fields. I remember the training we did together for my university degrees. I remember his love of food and how gentle he was with everyone he met. I remember him falling in the river and having to pull him out by his harness because the riverbank was so steep. I remember him chewing my doorframe as a puppy, and I remember feeding him cheeseburgers in his final few days. Most of all, I remember, and cherish, the relationship and connection that we had. This can never be taken from me – I will carry it forever.

What you are building today with your puppy is a relationship. It's a connection that will stay with you long after they are no longer physically here. Make sure it's a good one. Make your puppy's life one that you will look back on, maybe with a tear in your eye, but a big smile on your face. Above all, have fun.

I still feel you, Mr B.
~
I'm reminded of you
In everything I do
When I open the front door, I still feel you
When I walk to the kitchen, I still feel you
When I gaze out of the window, I still feel you
When I'm eating dinner, I still feel you
For you are eating dinner too
~
When I put on my shoes, I still feel you
When I put on my coat, I still feel you
When I step outside, I still feel you
When I walk in the park, I still feel you
When I walk by a stream, I still feel you
When I reach into my pocket, I still feel you
For you are looking to see if I have a treat or two.
~
When I awake each morning, I still feel you
When I leave the bathroom, I still feel you
When I pick up my phone, I still feel you
When I open the fridge, I still feel you
When I look at the bookshelf, I still feel you
When I log into Facebook, I still feel you
When I got my final grades, I could feel you
For it was you who earned those grades too
~
When I open my eyes, I still feel you
When I close my eyes, I still feel you
When I hear a noise, I still feel you
When I smell a smell, I still feel you
When I'm happy, I still feel you
When I'm sad, I still feel you
I cannot help but still feel you
In everything I do
For you are my eternal view
My everlasting memory of you

About the Author

Shay Kelly is a behaviour consultant with a passion for improving the life of companion dogs. He has studied canine behaviour and animal behaviour extensively, gaining FdSc and BSc in Canine Behaviour and Training, and a MSc in Applied Animal Behaviour and Training.

Shay's other books include:

Canine Enrichment: The book your dog needs you to read

Dog Training & Behaviour: a guide for everyone

Printed in Great Britain
by Amazon